SCIENCE to 14

Stephen Pople

OXFORD
UNIVERSITY PRESS

OXFORD
UNIVERSITY PRESS

Great Clarendon Street, Oxford OX2 6DP

Oxford University Press is a department of the University of Oxford.
It furthers the University's objective of excellence in research, scholarship,
and education by publishing worldwide in

Oxford New York

Athens Auckland Bangkok Bogotá Buenos Aires Calcutta
Cape Town Chennai Dar es Salaam Delhi Florence Hong Kong Istanbul
Karachi Kuala Lumpur Madrid Melbourne Mexico City Mumbai
Nairobi Paris São Paulo Singapore Taipei Tokyo Toronto Warsaw

with associated companies in Berlin Ibadan

Oxford is a registered trade mark of Oxford University Press
in the UK and in certain other countries

First published 1994
Reprinted 1994, 1995, 1996, 1997
2nd Edition published 2000

British Library Cataloguing in Publication Data

Data available

ISBN 0 19 914783 3

Printed in Spain by Gráficas Estella, S. A.

Acknowledgements

The publisher would like to thank the following for their kind permission to reproduce photographs:

p13 Science & Society Picture Library; p14 Science Photo Library/BSIP Laurent H Americain (top),
SPL/J Durham; p15 SPL/A&H Michler (top), Colorsport; p16 SPL/C Nuridsany & M Perennou; pp19, 20 Bruce
Coleman; p30 SPL/D Scharf; p32 SPL (all); p33 SPL/Custom Medical Stock Photo; p34 SPL/D G Settles;
p35 SPL/CNRI; p36 Oxford Scientific Films/A Bailey; p38 Animal Photography/Sally Anne Thompson;
p39 Colorsport; p40 Bruce Coleman; p42 Bruce Coleman/Kim Taylor; p43 Oxford Scientific Films/I West (left),
SPL/J Hesteltine (right), OSF (bottom left); p44 OSF/A Hay (left), /M Hamblin; p46 Zefa Photographic Library;
p47 J Allan Cash; p50 SPL/R Lappa (left), /S Ogden; p52 OSF/M Gibbs; p53 J Allan Cash; p56 Zefa;
p60 OSF/S Morris; p62 SPL/J Heseltine; p63 Colorific; p65 J Allan Cash; p67 Bruce Coleman (bottom), OSF
(right); p68 SPL/Rosenfield Images (left), J Allan Cash; p72 Dr A Waltham; p73 OSF/D Boag; pp74, 75 Dr A
Waltham, Geoscience Features/Dr B Booth; p76 SPL; p80 SPL/A Bartel; p83, 84 Allsport; p85 Ford UK;
p88 J Allan Cash; pp89, 90 Colorsport; p92 SPL/Photo Library International (bottom); p93 OSF/U Walz;
p94 SPL/J Amos; p96 J Allan Cash; p101, SPL/J Mead; p104 SPL/D Parker; p112 SPL/Astro Space (top left),
/National Snow & Ice Delta Services (top right), /NASA (bottom left), /D Parker (bottom right); p113 SPL/NASA

Cover photo: **PhotoDisc/Adalberto Rios Szalay/Sexto Sol**.

Additional photography by **Chris Honeywell**, **Peter Gould** & **Martin Sookias**.

The illustrations are by:

Chris Duggan, **Jeff Edwards**, **Jones Sewell**, **Pat Murray**, **Mike Ogden**,
Oxford Illustrators, **Pat Thorne**, **Borin Van Loon**, and **Pamela Venus**

Contents

Test and check (Sections 2–4) 5

1.01 Doing an investigation 8
1.02 Making measurements 10
1.03 Changing ideas 12
1.04 Products of science 14

2.01 Animals, plants, and cells 16
2.02 Making and using food 18
2.03 Seeds from cells 20
2.04 Action in the body 22
2.05 Bones, joints, and muscles 24
2.06 Food for the body 26
2.07 The lungs and breathing 28
2.08 Making human life 30
2.09 Growing to be born 32
2.10 Microbes and health 34
2.11 The variety of life 36
2.12 The same but different 38
2.13 Chains and webs 40
2.14 Adapted for living 42
2.15 Populations and problems 44

3.01 Looking at matter 46
3.02 Hot and cold 48
3.03 Elements, atoms, and compounds 50
3.04 Mixtures and solutions 52
3.05 More mixtures and solutions 54
3.06 Chemical and physical change 56
3.07 Acids and bases 58
3.08 More acids and bases 60
3.09 Burning 62

3.10 Metals and reactivity 64
3.11 More metals and reactivity 66
3.12 Made by reactions 68
3.13 The periodic table 70
3.14 Rocks and fragments 72
3.15 Forming rocks 74

4.01 Electricity on the move 76
4.02 Circuits and cells 78
4.03 Magnets and electromagnets 80
4.04 Forces 82
4.05 Moving and stopping 84
4.06 Pressure 86
4.07 Turning forces 88
4.08 Energy 90
4.09 Energy on the move 92
4.10 More energy on the move 94
4.11 Supplying the energy 96
4.12 How the world gets its energy 98
4.13 Sending sounds 100
4.14 Detecting sounds 102
4.15 Rays of light 104
4.16 Seeing colours 106
4.17 Sun and Earth 108
4.18 The Solar System 110
4.19 Satellites in orbit 112

Key ideas (Section 2–4) 114
Periodic table 117
Test questions (Sections 2–4) 118
Answers to questions 124
Index 127

Introduction

If you are working towards Key Stage 3 (levels 3 to 7) of the Science National Curriculum, then this book is designed for you. It explains the science concepts that you will meet, and helps you find what you need to know. The topics are covered in double-page units which we have called **spreads**. To help you with the text, most spreads have a list of **key words** near the beginning.

Contents Here, you can see how the spreads are arranged.

Test and check Try answering these questions when you revise. At the end of each question, there is a number telling you which spread to look up if you need to check information or find out more.

Spreads 1.01 to 1.04 These deal with scientific enquiry and relate to Attainment Target 1 of the Science National Curriculum. They should help you plan and carry out investigations, discover how scientists' ideas can change, and find out how science can lead to the development of new products.

Spreads 2.01 to 4.19 These are grouped into three sections, matching Attainment Targets 2, 3, and 4 of the Science National Curriculum:

Section 2: Life processes and living things (Attainment Target 2)

Section 3: Materials and their properties (Attainment Target 3)

Section 4: Physical processes (Attainment Target 4)

Key ideas These are summaries of the main ideas in each section, grouped as in the Science National Curriculum.

Test questions These are practice questions to help you prepare for you Key Stage 3 Science tests.

Answers to questions Here, you will find brief answers to all the questions in the spreads and tests, not just the numerical ones. But try the questions before you look at the answers!

Index Use this if you have a particular scientific word or term which you need to look up.

The book should support your scientific enquiries and help you understand scientific ideas. I hope that you will find it useful.

Test and check

Can you answer the following? The spread number in brackets tells you where to find the information.

1 In an animal or plant, what are tissues and organs made of? *(2.01)*
2 Which part of a cell is the 'control centre'? *(2.01)*
3 What type of cell has chloroplasts in it? What do chloroplasts do? *(2.01)*
4 What type of cell has a cell wall? What does the cell wall do? *(2.01)*
5 How do plants obtain their food? What is the process called? *(2.02)*
6 Why do plants need nitrogen? *(2.02)*
7 How do plants and animals get their energy? What is the process called? *(2.02)*
8 Why does the world not run out of oxygen? *(2.02)*
9 In a flower, where are the male sex cells and female sex cells stored? *(2.03)*
10 In a flower, what happens during fertilization? *(2.03)*
11 How are the organs of your body supplied with the food and other materials they need? *(2.04)*
12 What are the three main jobs done by your skeleton? *(2.05)*
13 Why do muscles work in pairs? *(2.05)*
14 What are the seven different types of substance you need in a balanced diet? *(2.06)*
15 When you chew your food, what does the enzyme amylase do? *(2.06)*
16 What happens to food during digestion? *(2.06)*
17 What happens to food which has been digested? *(2.06)*
18 In the lungs, what substances enter the blood? What substances are removed from the blood? *(2.07)*
19 In the lungs, what are alveoli? *(2.07)*
20 In the lungs, what are cilia, and what do they do? *(2.07)*
21 Can you write a word equation to describe what happens during aerobic respiration? *(2.07)*
22 How often do a woman's ovaries release an ovum? *(2.08)*
23 In humans, how is an ovum fertilized? What happens to it if it is fertilized? *(2.08)*
24 What happens if the ovum is not fertilized? *(2.08)*

25 In the uterus, how does a developing baby get its food and oxygen? *(2.09)*
26 Why should a woman avoid smoking when she is pregnant? *(2.09)*
27 What are germs? How can they spread from one person to another? *(2.10)*
28 How does your body defend itself against germs? *(2.10)*
29 What are vaccines, and what do they do? *(2.10)*
30 What feature do vertebrates have in common? *(2.11)*
31 What are the five main groups of vertebrates? *(2.11)*
32 Can you give two examples of inherited characteristics? *(2.12)*
33 Where is information about your inherited characteristics stored? *(2.12)*
34 Can you give an example of a characteristic which is affected by environmental factors? *(2.12)*
35 Can you give an example of selective breeding? *(2.12)*
36 Can you give an example of a food chain? *(2.13)*
37 Can you identify the producers and consumers in food chains? *(2.13)*
38 What is a pyramid of numbers? *(2.13)*
39 What is a food web? *(2.13)*
40 Can you explain how toxic chemicals can accumulate in a food chain? *(2.13)*
41 What is meant by the habitat of an animal or plant? *(2.14)*
42 Can you give an example of how an animal or plant is adapted to its environment? *(2.14)*
43 Can you give an example of how the environment of an animal or plant might change from one season to another? *(2.14)*
44 Humans grow crops. How can this affect other populations of plants and animals? *(2.15)*
45 Can you give three factors which would limit the size of a population of animals? *(2.15)*
46 Can you give three factors which would limit the size of a population of plants? *(2.15)*
47 What is meant by sustainable development? *(2.15)*

Test and check

Can you answer the following? The spread number in brackets tells you where to find the information.

1 According to the particle theory of matter, how do the particles behave in a solid, in a liquid, and in a gas? *(3.01)*

2 What is meant by the density of a material? *(3.01)*

3 How does the particle theory of matter explain...
...diffusion?
...gas pressure? *(3.01)*

4 What is meant by the melting point of a substance, and the boiling point? *(3.02)*

5 Can you give an example of a change of state? *(3.02)*

6 What happens to a liquid when it evaporates? *(3.02)*

7 What are the two main types of element? *(3.03)*

8 What is the smallest bit of an element? *(3.03)*

9 What is the difference between an element and a compound? *(3.03)*

10 What does the chemical formula H_2O tell you about water? *(3.03)*

11 What is the difference between a mixture and a compound? *(3.04)*

12 What is a solute? What is a solvent? What is a solution? *(3.04)*

13 What is meant by a saturated solution? *(3.04)*

14 What factors affect solubility? *(3.04)*

15 What is an alloy? Why are alloys made? *(3.04)*

16 What are the two main gases in air? What are they used for? *(3.05)*

17 How would you separate...
...sand from salt?
...copper sulphate from water?
...the different inks in a mixture? *(3.05)*

18 Can you give an example of a chemical change? *(3.06)*

19 How can you tell whether a chemical change has taken place? *(3.06)*

20 Can you give an example of a physical change? *(3.06)*

21 What happens to the total mass of material during a chemical or physical change? *(3.06)*

22 What gas is given off when an acid reacts with a metal? *(3.07)*

23 How does an acid affect litmus indicator? *(3.07)*

24 How does an alkali affect litmus indicator? *(3.07)*

25 What type of solution has...
...a pH of 1?
...a pH of 7?
...a pH of 14? *(3.07)*

26 Can you give three examples of a base (such as an alkali) being used to neutralize an acid? *(3.08)*

27 If a base neutralizes an acid what are the products? *(3.08)*

28 If an acid reacts with a carbonate, what are the products? *(3.08)*

29 If an element burns in oxygen, what is the product? *(3.09)*

30 What is the combustion triangle? *(3.09)*

31 Can you describe a test for oxygen? *(3.09)*

32 Can you describe a test for carbon dioxide? *(3.09)*

33 What problems are caused by burning fossil fuels? *(3.09)*

34 What does the reactivity series tell you about different metals? *(3.10)*

35 Why is gold found in the ground as a pure metal, while iron is only found in compounds? *(3.10)*

36 Can you give an example of a displacement reaction? *(3.11)*

37 Can you give an example of a reaction in which metals compete for oxygen? *(3.11)*

38 What has happened on the surface of a metal if it has become corroded? *(3.11)*

39 Can you give three examples of useful materials made by chemical reactions? *(3.12)*

40 Can you give an example of food oxidation? *(3.12)*

41 What does the periodic table show? *(3.13)*

42 Can you describe two ways in which a rock may become weathered? *(3.14)*

43 Can you explain how fragments from one rock can end up in another rock? *(3.14)*

44 How are igneous rocks formed? *(3.15)*

45 Why do some igneous rocks have larger crysals that others? *(3.15)*

46 How are sedimentary rocks formed? *(3.15)*

47 How are metamorphic rocks formed? *(3.15)*

Test and check

Can you answer the following? The spread number in brackets tells you where to find the information.

1 Which materials are the best conductors of electricity? *(4.01)*

2 Can you draw a simple circuit with a cell, a bulb, and a switch in it? *(4.01)*

3 How does a switch stop a current flowing? *(4.01)*

4 What instruments would you use to measure current and voltage? *(4.02)*

5 Can you draw a circuit with a cell and two bulbs in series? What would be the effect of using two cells in series instead of one? *(4.02)*

6 Can you draw a circuit with a cell and two bulbs in parallel? What are the advantages of the parallel arrangement? *(4.02)*

7 Can you draw circuits using symbols? *(4.02)*

8 What happens when like poles of two magnets are brought close? *(4.03)*

9 Can you sketch the magnetic field round a bar magnet? *(4.03)*

10 Can you describe three uses of electromagnets? *(4.03)*

11 Why should the core of an electromagnet be made of iron rather than steel? *(4.03)*

12 How would you measure a force? *(4.04)*

13 What is 'weight'? *(4.04)*

14 What are the forces on a parachutist descending at steady speed? How do they compare? *(4.04)*

15 If the forces on something are unbalanced, how will this affect its motion? *(4.04)*

16 How do you calculate speed? *(4.05)*

17 Can you give two ways in which friction is useful and two ways in which it is a nuisance? *(4.05)*

18 How do you calculate pressure? *(4.06)*

19 Can you give an example of something which...
...reduces the pressure on the ground?
...increases the pressure on the ground? *(4.06)*

20 If you are pulling on a spanner, how could you increase the turning effect of the force? *(4.07)*

21 What is meant by the moment of a force? *(4.07)*

22 What is the law of moments? *(4.07)*

23 Can you give three examples of things which store energy? *(4.08)*

24 What is the law of conservation of energy? *(4.08)*

25 What is the difference between heat and temperature? *(4.09)*

26 Can you give three ways in which heat can be transferred from one place to another? *(4.09, 4.10)*

27 Why are wool and fur good insulators? *(4.09)*

28 What is the difference between a renewable and a non-renewable energy source? Can you give an example of each type? *(4.11)*

29 Can you describe how different energy sources can be used to generate electricity? *(4.11, 4.12)*

30 Can you explain why the Sun is the source of most of our energy? *(4.11, 4.12)*

31 What causes sound waves? *(4.13)*

32 Why cannot sound travel through a vacuum? *(4.13)*

33 How does the speed of sound compare with the speed of light? *(4.13)*

34 How does your ear detect sound? *(4.14)*

35 Comparing sound waves, how are loud sounds different from quiet sounds? How are high sounds different from low sounds? *(4.14)*

36 Why are loud sounds harmful? *(4.14)*

37 Why do the letters on this page look darker than the paper? *(4.15)*

38 How is a ray of light reflected by a flat mirror? *(4.15)*

39 How does a flat mirror form an image? *(4.15)*

40 What happens to a ray of light when it enters glass at an angle? What is the effect called? *(4.15)*

41 What happens to white light when it passes through a prism? *(4.16)*

42 What primary colours must be added to make white? *(4.16)*

43 What colour(s) does a red filter transmit? What colour(s) does it absorb? *(4.16)*

44 Why do we get day and night? *(4.17)*

45 Why does the Sun's motion across the sky appear to change during the year? *(4.17)*

46 What planets are there in the Solar System? *(4.18)*

47 What holds the planets in orbit around the Sun? *(4.18)*

48 Can you give three different uses of satellites? *(4.19)*

Doing an investigation

This spread should help you to
- plan an experimental investigation
- obtain and present your evidence
- consider your evidence
- evaluate your investigation.

The right-hand side of each page shows one student's thoughts about her investigation.

Planning

● **Decide on a problem to investigate**

In the example shown on the right, the student has decided to investigate how quickly sugar dissolves in water.

● **Write down your prediction**

You may already have an idea of what you expect to happen in your investigation. This is your **prediction**. It may not be right! The aim of your investigation is to test it.

● **Decide what the key factors are**

The **key factors** are those things which can affect the outcome of your experiment. For example, in sugar-dissolving tests, two of the key factors are how much water you use, and whether you stir the mixture or not. In your experiment, you must decide what the key factors are, and which ones you can control. Of those, which will you keep fixed, and which will you change?

● **Check that your tests will be fair**

To make sense of your results, you need to change just one factor at a time and find out how it affects one other. Otherwise, it will not be a **fair test**. For example, if you want to find out how the crystal size affects dissolving, it wouldn't be fair to compare big, brown sugar crystals in hot water with small, white ones in cold water.

● **Decide what equipment you need, and in what order you will do things**

To help in your planning, you may need to carry out a trial run of the experiment.

● **Prepare tables for your results**

First, decide how what readings you will take, how many of them, and over what range.

prediction   key factor   fair test
line of best fit

I will investigate how quickly sugar dissolves in water.

Sugar is made up of tiny crystals. In icing sugar, the crystals are very small. In caster sugar, they are a bit bigger. In ordinary sugar, they are a bit bigger again.

If the crystals are small, the water can get in contact with all the sugar more quickly. So I think that small crystals will dissolve more quickly than bigger ones.

I also think that sugar particles will dissolve more quickly in hot water....

Three of the key factors are:
    time for the sugar to dissolve
    particle size
    temperature

Other key factors are the amount of sugar, the amount of water, the type of sugar (brown or white), and whether I stir it or not. I will use the same amounts of sugar and water each time. I will use white sugar, and I will stir it gently to separate the crystals. If the crystals are in a heap, the water cannot reach them properly.

Items need:
ordinary sugar, caster sugar, icing sugar, beaker, thermometer.....

8

First, I will find out how temperature affects dissolving. I will use ordinary sugar each time, so that the crystal size is fixed. I will dissolve the sugar in water at different temperatures. I will measure the temperature with a thermometer, and the time for dissolving with a stopwatch.

Next, I will see how crystal size affects dissolving. I might be able to measure the size of the sugar crystals with a microscope. If not, I will just call them 'small', 'medium', and 'large'.

Obtaining and presenting evidence

● **Make your measurements and record them**
For greater accuracy, repeat measurements.

● **Present your results**
Decide whether it would be useful to show them in the form of a chart or graph (see below).

Considering your evidence

● **Look for patterns in your results**
A graph shows how one factor changes with another. Some measurements are difficult to make accurately, so the points on your graph may be uneven. Draw a ***line of best fit*** through them. This is the straight line or smooth curve which passes close to as many points as possible.

● **Present your conclusions**
What links did you find between the factors you measured? Can you explain these links? Did your results match your prediction?

Evaluating your investigation

● **Evaluate your evidence**
Did you get enough data to reach firm conclusions? Did any of your measurements seem to be 'wrong'? If so, can you explain why?

● **Evaluate your methods**
Could your experiment be improved in any way?

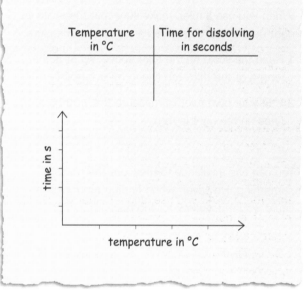

Temperature in °C	Time for dissolving in seconds

There seems to be a link between time for dissolving and temperature. As the temperature gets higher, the time for dissolving gets........

This is why I think there is a link. When the temperature rises...........

Measuring the time accurately was difficult. It was hard to tell when all the sugar had dissolved. Also, I would like to measure the crystal size more accurately.

Making measurements

This spread should help you to:
- *take readings on measuring instruments.*

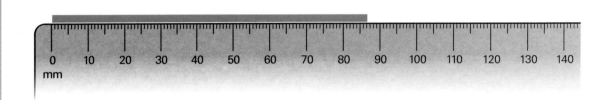

When you use a ruler, make sure that the scale is right next to the object you are trying to measure.

1 Read the scale on the ruler above. What is the length of the thick red line in millimetres (mm)?

2 Use your own ruler to measure the lengths of the lines on the right in mm.

A

B

You can use a balance to measure the mass of something. However, when finding the mass of a liquid, you must allow for the mass of its container.

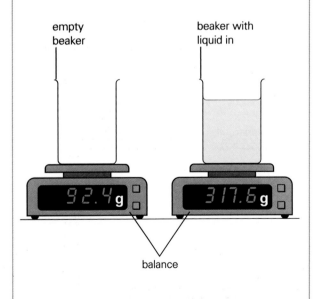

empty beaker

beaker with liquid in

balance

3 What is the mass of the liquid in the beaker above in grams (g)?

You can use a measuring cylinder to find the volume of a liquid. When you take the reading:
– the measuring cylinder must be upright, so make sure that it is resting on a level table or bench
– you must look at the level of the liquid's flat surface on the scale, and not its curved edge.

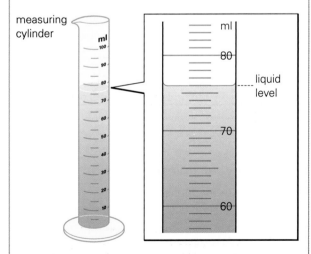

measuring cylinder

liquid level

4 What is the volume of the liquid in the measuring cylinder above in millilitres (ml)?

Weights and other forces can be measured using a spring balance. Two types are shown below. Both are marked in units called newtons (N).

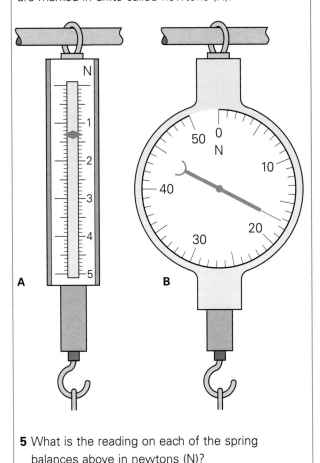

A

B

5 What is the reading on each of the spring balances above in newtons (N)?

When using a thermometer to measure the temperature of a liquid:
– keep the liquid well stirred
– give the thermometer time to reach the right temperature
– keep the bulb of the thermometer in the liquid while you take the reading.

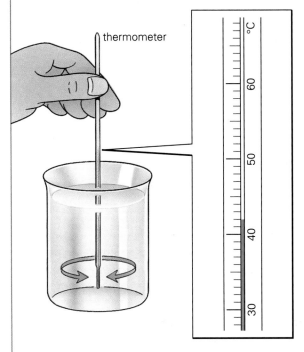

6 What is the reading on the thermometer above in degrees Celsius (°C)?

Some meters give a digital reading: they display a number. Others have a pointer which moves along a scale, like the ones below.

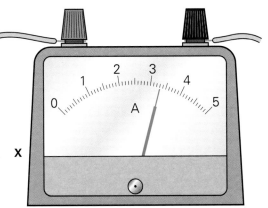

X

When reading meters like those below, make sure that you look at the pointer and scale 'square on'. The pointer may have a flat end to help you do this.

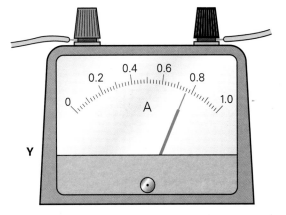

Y

7 What is the reading on each of the meters above in amperes (A)?

Changing ideas

By the end of this spread, you should be able to:
- *explain how scientists develop explanations based on models, and then test their ideas.*

Scientific ideas can change as more and more experimental evidence is collected. Here is an example – people's ideas about the Universe and Earth's place within it. This is our present view:

> The Earth is a planet, one of several orbiting (moving around) the Sun. The Sun is a star. It is a member of a huge group of billions of stars called a galaxy. There are billions of galaxies in the Universe. They appear to be moving apart. They were created in a gigantic explosion called the Big Bang which happened billions of years ago.

No one can be sure that the above description is correct in every detail. It is just a useful picture – scientists call it a **model**. It matches the observations and measurements that we now have. It has taken many centuries to develop and is very different from earlier models. This is its story:

c. = *circa* (about)

350 BC   Aristotle believes that the Earth is at the centre of the Universe. Heavenly bodies such as the Sun, Moon, and stars lie on transparent crystal spheres which revolve about it. The motion of the bodies is eternal, unchanging, and in perfect circles. This model is based on Ancient Greek beliefs about the perfection of the heavens rather than on accurate observations.

AD

c. 150   Ptolemy realises that the motion of a planet can appear to wobble. He does not want to abandon the idea of perfect circles, so he develops a complicated model of orbits with little circles added to bigger ones. He keeps the Earth at the centre.

KEY WORD

model

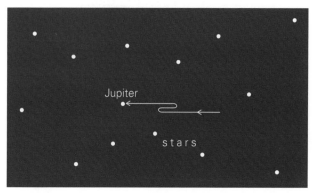

Viewed from Earth, the planet Jupiter shows a wobble in its motion. It doesn't really go backwards. It only appears to do so because our viewpoint changes as the Earth moves round the Sun.

1543   Nicolaus Copernicus suggests a new model to explain the observed motion of the planets. The Earth is a planet and, with the other planets, orbits the Sun. His ideas are rejected.

1608   The telescope is invented. Later, Galileo makes observations which indicate that the Earth is not at the centre of the Universe.

1609   Johannes Kepler analyses a huge number of astronomical measurements made by Tycho Brahe. He deduces that planets must orbit the Sun in ellipses or circles.

1687   Newton publishes his theory of gravitation and laws of motion. He is able to explain why planets orbit in the way they do.

c. 1790   William Herschel, aided by his sister Caroline, makes a careful survey of the stars. He concludes that they are arranged in a huge group which he calls the Galaxy. He estimates that the Sun, which is also a star, is at the centre of the Galaxy.

When Herschel built this telescope in 1789, it was the biggest and best in the world.

1918   By now, greatly improved telescopes mean that astronomers can make much more detailed observations of distant stars. Harlow Shapley maps the positions of the stars in the Galaxy and concludes that the Sun is not at its centre after all.

1923   Edwin Hubble discovers that there are many more galaxies besides our own. Their shapes can be elliptical, spiral, or irregular.

1929   Edwin Hubble analyses the light from distant galaxies. His results suggest that the galaxies are moving apart. We seem to be living in an expanding Universe.

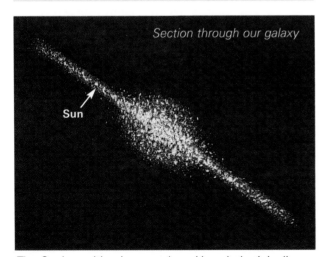

Section through our galaxy

Sun

The Sun's position in our galaxy. Herschel originally thought that the Sun was near the centre.

Today   The most widely-accepted model of the Universe is based on the Big Bang theory. It explains why the galaxies are moving apart:

Between 10 and 20 billion years ago, the whole of space and everything in it exploded from a tiny concentration of matter and energy. This was the Big Bang. It created the matter from which the galaxies would form. They have been moving apart ever since.

◦ Big Bang

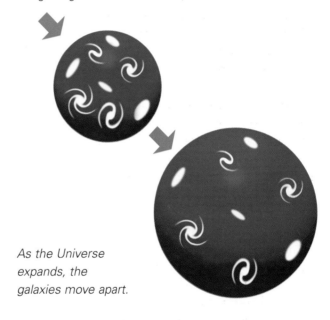

As the Universe expands, the galaxies move apart.

The future   Will the Universe go on expanding for ever? Why did it start to expand in the first place?

To answer questions like this, scientists do not always need to look into space. The Big Bang created the different atomic particles from which all matter is made. Scientists are developing models to explain how these particles are related. They use their models to predict how the particles will behave, then test their ideas with experiments. This should help them explain how the Universe began and what will happen to it in the future.

Products of science

By the end of this spread, you should be able to:
- give examples of how science has led to the development of products which are useful in everyday life or can help the environment.

KEY WORDS

product (anything manufactured, or produced naturally)
environment (our surroundings, or the conditions in which we live)

New products often come from scientific discoveries. Here are some examples:

Lasers

Physicist Theodore Maiman built the first laser in 1960. He found a way of energizing a specially-cut crystal so that it produced an intense, narrow beam of light. Here are some of the uses of lasers:

Bar code readers scan labels with a beam from a tiny laser. Pulses of reflected light are picked up and processed by a computer, which displays the price.

CD players contain a tiny laser. Pulses reflected from the spinning disc inside are picked up and processed to give sounds, pictures, or computer data.

Optical fibre cables carry digital telephone signals in the form of pulses of laser light.

Laser scalpels are used by surgeons to make very fine cuts which also seal the tissue.

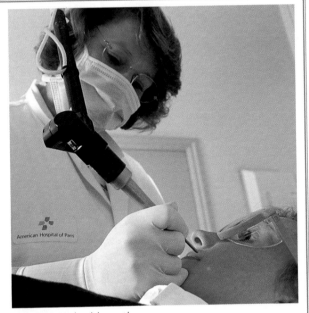

A laser scalpel in action

Antibiotics

Diseases such as sore throats, typhoid, dysentry, and pneumonia are caused by microscopic living things known as bacteria (or germs). Antibiotics are medicines which can damage or kill bacteria.

Penicillin was the first major antibiotic. It was discovered in 1928, by accident, by Alexander Fleming. While working in his laboratory, he noticed that mould had grown on a dish containing bacteria. Something in the mould was killing the bacteria. He extracted the substance and called it penicillin.

Today, there are hundreds of antibiotics. They have revolutionized the treatment of bacterial diseases, but doctors know that they must be used sparingly. When antibiotics kill off germs, new and more resistant forms of the germ can develop.

Bacteria (light brown) grow on a jelly in a dish. The dark area shows where bacteria have been killed by a pellet of penicillin (white) placed in the middle.

Catalysts

During chemical reactions, substances break up or combine to form new substances. Scientists have discovered that some materials can trigger or speed up chemical reactions. They call them catalysts. Catalysts are used in the production of a whole range of chemicals, fuels, and plastics from crude oil and natural gas. They are also used to change polluting gases from car engines into less polluting ones.

With catalysts, hydrogen can be extracted from less explosive fuels such as methanol. This may be useful in the future, when electric cars eventually replace petrol and diesel ones. Electric cars could carry methanol in their tanks as a source of hydrogen to power their fuel cells (batteries). The only exhaust gas coming from a hydrogen-powered car would be water vapour.

This catalytic converter is part of a car's exhaust system. It 'cleans up' the exhaust fumes by changing polluting gases into less polluting ones.

Most high-performance fabrics are made from plastic fibres, although natural fibres, such as cotton, may also be mixed in.

Plastics

Chemist Alexander Parkes invented the first plastic in 1862. He called it Parkesine. Later plastics included celluloid (1869), Bakelite (1909), Perspex (1930), and nylon (1935). Modern plastics can be produced in lumps, tubes, sheets, films, or fibres that can be woven into fabrics. Most are made by chemical processes that start with crude oil.

Plastics can be bad for the environment. If thrown away, they lie around without rotting away. To deal with this problem, scientists are trying to develop plastics that can be broken up by bacteria.

1 Name a product used today which you think may have come from each of these discoveries:
a) In 1835, James Bowman Lindsay found that an electric current could make a thin wire heat up and glow.
b) In 1895, William Roentgen discovered an invisible radiation which could penetrate flesh but be picked up by photographic film.

2 Some products are useful to us, but harmful to the environment. Petrol engines are an example. Using information from this spread and your own ideas:
a) give *two* more examples of products which are harmful to the environment.
b) give *two* examples of products which can help improve the environment.

2.01 Animals, plants, and cells

By the end of this spread, you should be able to:
- *explain what cells are*
- *describe the differences between animal cells and plant cells.*

Animals and plants need food for energy and growth. But they get their food in different ways:

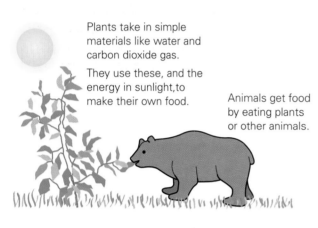

Plants take in simple materials like water and carbon dioxide gas.

They use these, and the energy in sunlight, to make their own food.

Animals get food by eating plants or other animals.

Animals and plants are made from tiny **cells**. Cells are microscopic chemical factories where the vital processes of life take place. They take in substances, make new ones, release energy from food, and give out waste.

Animals and plants grow by **cell division**. A cell splits to form two new cells. Then these split... and so on. You started as a single cell, but there are billions of cells in your body now.

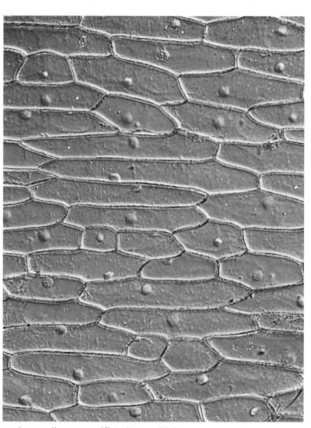

onion cells: magnification ×500

Animal cells

Animal cells exist in many shapes and sizes. But they all have several features in common:

Nucleus This controls all the chemical reactions that take place in the cell. It contains, thread-like **chromosomes** which store the chemical instructions needed to build the cell and make it do its job.

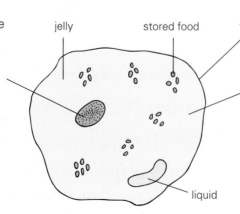

jelly   stored food   liquid

Cell membrane This is a thin skin which controls the movement of materials in and out of the cell.

Cytoplasm In this jelly, the cell's vital chemical reactions take place. New substances are made, and energy is released and stored. Sometimes, cytoplasm contains tiny droplets of liquid called **vacuoles**.

Plant cells

Plant cells also have a **cell membrane**, **cytoplasm**, and **nucleus**. But they have some features which make them different from animal cells:

Cell wall Plant cells are surrounded by a firm wall made of **cellulose**. This holds plant cells together and gives them much of their strength. For example, wood is mainly cellulose.

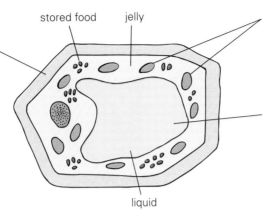

stored food   jelly

liquid

Chloroplasts These contain a green substance called **chlorophyll**. This absorbs the energy in sunlight. Plants need the energy to make their food.

Cell sap This is a watery liquid in a large vacuole. Pressure from the liquid keeps the cell firm, rather like a tiny balloon. If a plant loses too much liquid from its cells, the pressure falls and the plant wilts.

Groups of cells

In animals and plants, different groups of cells have different jobs to do. Groups of similar cells are called **tissue**. A collection of tissues doing a particular job is an **organ**. Eyes are organs, so are muscles.

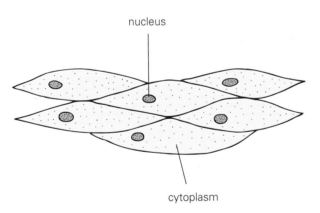

nucleus

cytoplasm

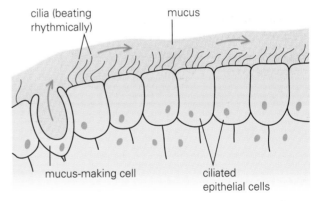

cilia (beating rhythmically)   mucus

mucus-making cell   ciliated epithelial cells

The muscles in your arms and legs are made from cells like this. The cells can shorten so that the muscle contracts.

Your nose is lined with cells like this to 'clean' the air. The mucus traps dust and germs. The tiny cilia (hairs) push the mucus along to your throat.

---

1 *nucleus   cellulose   membrane   chloroplast   cytoplasm*

Which of the above matches each of these?
a) Absorbs the energy in sunlight.
b) The walls of plant cells are made of this.
c) The part of a cell where new substances are made and energy is stored and released.
d) A thin skin around the cytoplasm.
e) A cell's control centre.

2 Animals and plants need food.
a) Give *two* reasons why animals and plants need food.
b) How do animals get their food?
c) How do plants get their food?

3 Give *two* features which plant cells have but animal cells do not.

4 a) What is tissue? **b)** What word means a collection of tissues doing one particular job?

Making and using food

By the end of this spread, you should be able to:
- explain how plants make their food
- explain why animals and plants respire
- name the gases involved in making and using food.

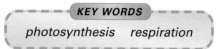

Living things need food. It supplies them with energy, and materials for growth. Animals have to find their food, but plants make their own.

Photosynthesis

Plants take in carbon dioxide gas from the air, and water from the soil. They use the energy in sunlight to turn these into food such as glucose sugar, as shown on the right. The process is called **photosynthesis**. It also produces oxygen gas.

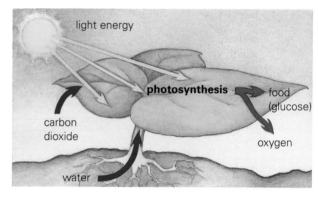

Stem contains cells which form tubes:

tubes for carrying water and dissolved minerals

tubes for carrying dissolved food

water evaporates

Veins contain cells which form tubes

Water and dissolved minerals flow from roots to leaves

Dissolved food flows from leaves to storage areas, growing points, or wherever it is needed

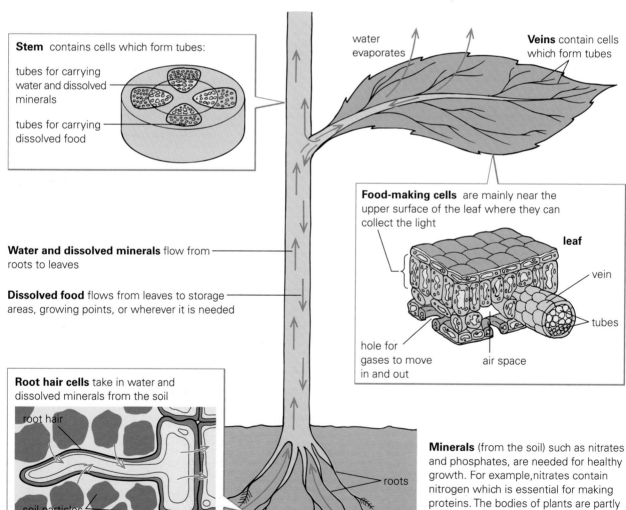

Food-making cells are mainly near the upper surface of the leaf where they can collect the light

leaf

vein

tubes

hole for gases to move in and out

air space

Root hair cells take in water and dissolved minerals from the soil

root hair

soil particles

roots

Minerals (from the soil) such as nitrates and phosphates, are needed for healthy growth. For example, nitrates contain nitrogen which is essential for making proteins. The bodies of plants are partly built from proteins.

To absorb the energy in sunlight, plants have a green chemical called chlorophyll in their leaves.

Photosynthesis can be summarized by this equation:

$$\text{carbon dioxide} + \text{water} \xrightarrow{\text{light energy}} \text{glucose} + \text{oxygen}$$

Plants need only some of the oxygen they make. The rest comes out through tiny holes in their leaves. The carbon dioxide comes in through the same holes.

When plants make their food, they can store it in their leaves and roots to be used later on. Some is stored in the form of **starch**. When animals eat plants, they are eating this stored food.

Respiration

Plants and animals get energy from their food by a chemical process called **respiration**. It is rather like burning, but without any flames. Usually, the food is combined with oxygen from the air. As energy is released, carbon dioxide and water are made. The air you breathe out contains extra carbon dioxide and water produced by respiration.

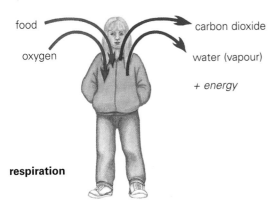

food → carbon dioxide
oxygen → water (vapour)
+ energy

respiration

Respiration using oxygen is called **aerobic respiration**. It can be summarized by this equation:

$$\text{food} + \text{oxygen} \rightarrow \text{carbon dioxide} + \text{water} + \text{energy}$$

Gases in balance

During daylight hours, plants make more oxygen than they need. At night, photosynthesis stops, so plants must take in oxygen – just like animals. However, plants use less oxygen during the night than they give out during the day.

Overall, plants take in carbon dioxide and give out oxygen, while animals take in oxygen and give out carbon dioxide. Between them, they keep the gases in the atmosphere in balance.

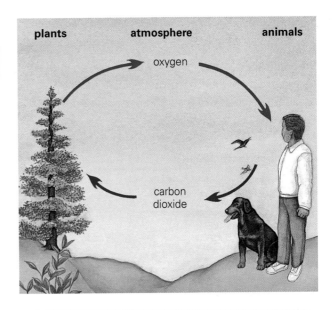

1 *carbon dioxide   nitrogen   oxygen*
   Which of the above is
   a) taken in by plants during photosynthesis?
   b) produced by plants during photosynthesis?
   c) used up during respiration?
   d) produced during respiration?
2 Apart from 1 b) above, what else do plants make during photosynthesis?
3 Why does photosynthesis usually stop at night?
4 What are *stomata*, and what are they used for?
5 What are *root hair cells* used for?
6 Animals are using up oxygen all the time. Why does the amount of oxygen in the atmosphere not go down?

Seeds from cells

By the end of this spread, you should be able to:
- describe where the sex cells are in a flower
- describe what happens during fertilization
- explain how seeds are formed.

Many plants have flowers. Flowers produce the seeds which will grow into new plants. But before a seed can develop, a **male sex cell** must combine with a **female sex cell**, as on the right.

Inside a flower

Some flowers contain male sex cells. Some contain female sex cells. But many contain both types.

Stamens hold the grains of **pollen** which contain the male sex cells. Pollen in released when the **anther** ripens and splits open.

Carpels have a space inside called an **ovary**. In the ovary are tiny **ovules**, each containing a female sex cell. Carpels also have a sticky tip called a **stigma**. Pollen can stick to this.

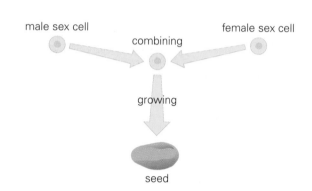

male sex cell   female sex cell

combining

growing

seed

Parts of a flower

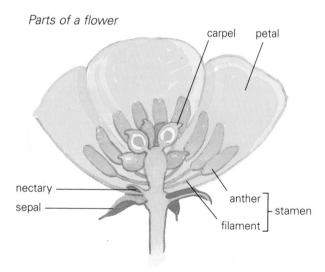

carpel   petal

nectary

sepal

anther ⎤
        ⎥ stamen
filament ⎦

Anther: lower half

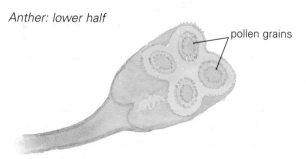

pollen grains

Pollination

Before a male sex cell can combine with a female sex cell, pollen must get across to a stigma and stick to it. This is called **pollination**. Usually, the pollen is carried across to another flower.

Some flowers are pollinated by insects. The insects are attracted by the scent or bright colours. As they search for sugary nectar inside the flower, they get covered in pollen, which they carry to other flowers.

Some flowers are pollinated by wind. Their flowers are often small and dull, but their stamens hang out so that pollen can be blown across to other flowers. Grasses are wind-pollinated. When their pollen blows about, you may get 'hay fever'.

Fertilization

When a pollen grain sticks to a stigma, a pollen tube may grow out of the grain and down to an ovule. A nucleus from a male sex cell can pass down this tube and combine with the nucleus of the female sex cell. If this happens, the cell has been **fertilized**.

Seeds and fruits

A complete ovary after fertilization is called a **fruit**. In the ovary, each fertilized cell grows by cell division to form a seed.

Plants try to scatter their seeds over a large area so that some may survive to grow into new plants. Different plants use different methods of **dispersal**:

- Some seeds have hooks so that they can be carried by animals.
- Some fruits are eaten by animals. The seeds come out with the droppings.
- Some seeds are shaped so that they can be carried by the wind.
- Some seeds are in pods. These pop open when dry and flick out the seeds.

Germination

If a seed absorbs water, and the temperature and air conditions are right, it may begin to grow. A tiny shoot grows upwards, and a root grows downwards, Scientists say that the seed has **germinated**.

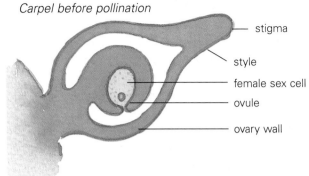

Carpel before pollination

stigma
style
female sex cell
ovule
ovary wall

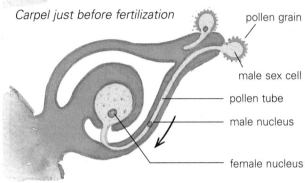

Carpel just before fertilization

pollen grain
male sex cell
pollen tube
male nucleus
female nucleus

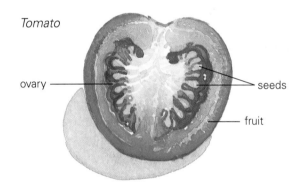

Tomato

ovary
seeds
fruit

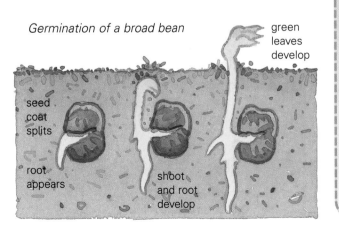

Germination of a broad bean

green leaves develop
seed coat splits
root appears
shoot and root develop

1 Which part of a flower contains **a)** the female sex cells **b)** the male sex cells?

2 *fertilization   pollination   germination*
   Which of the above means
   a) transfer of pollen from one flower to another?
   b) a seed developing a root and a shoot?
   c) a male sex cell combining with a female sex cell?

3 In a flower, what does an ovary become after fertilization?

4 Explain the following:
   a) Many flowers are brightly coloured.
   b) Some fruits develop in such a way that they are tempting for animals to eat.

2.04 Action in the body

By the end of this spread, you should be able to:
- *explain why the body needs to take in some materials and get rid of others*
- *describe what different organs of the body do.*

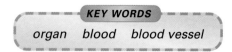
An **organ** is any part of the body with a special job to do. The next page shows some of the main organs of the human body. The organs are made of cells.

Heart and blood

Your heart pumps blood round the body through a system of tubes called **blood vessels**. Blood leaves the heart through **arteries** and returns through **veins**. These are linked by networks of very narrow tubes called **capillaries**. Every cell in the body is close to a capillary, so blood can bring new materials to the cell and take waste products away.

Carried in the blood

Your body takes in oxygen, water, and food (which it changes into liquid form). The blood carries these to cells in all your organs. Each cell is a tiny chemical factory. It uses some incoming materials to make new substances for growth and repair, and others to get energy by respiration (see Spread 2.02).

Respiration produces carbon dioxide and water. The blood carries these and other waste products to the organs that get rid of them. Your body also has other waste – unused food that goes right through you.

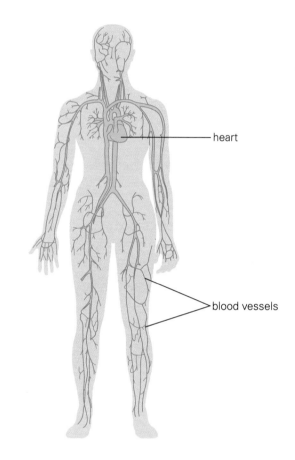

heart

blood vessels

Some of the blood vessels in the human body

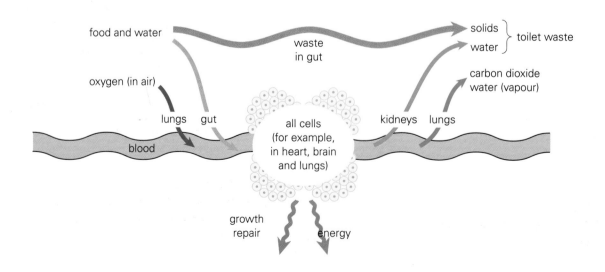

food and water

solids ⎱
water ⎰ toilet waste

waste in gut

oxygen (in air)

carbon dioxide water (vapour)

lungs   gut

kidneys   lungs

all cells (for example, in heart, brain and lungs)

blood

growth repair   energy

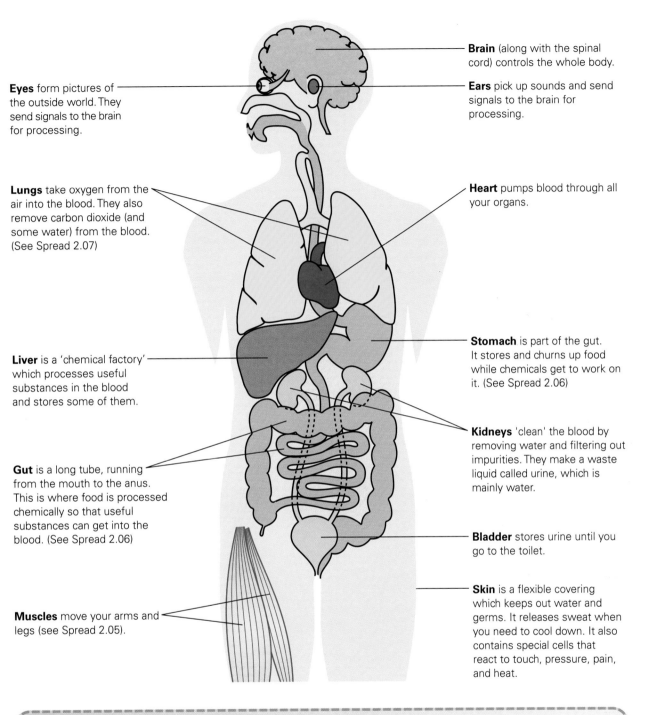

Eyes form pictures of the outside world. They send signals to the brain for processing.

Brain (along with the spinal cord) controls the whole body.

Ears pick up sounds and send signals to the brain for processing.

Lungs take oxygen from the air into the blood. They also remove carbon dioxide (and some water) from the blood. (See Spread 2.07)

Heart pumps blood through all your organs.

Liver is a 'chemical factory' which processes useful substances in the blood and stores some of them.

Stomach is part of the gut. It stores and churns up food while chemicals get to work on it. (See Spread 2.06)

Kidneys 'clean' the blood by removing water and filtering out impurities. They make a waste liquid called urine, which is mainly water.

Gut is a long tube, running from the mouth to the anus. This is where food is processed chemically so that useful substances can get into the blood. (See Spread 2.06)

Bladder stores urine until you go to the toilet.

Skin is a flexible covering which keeps out water and germs. It releases sweat when you need to cool down. It also contains special cells that react to touch, pressure, pain, and heat.

Muscles move your arms and legs (see Spread 2.05).

---

1 stomach   lung   heart   kidney
liver   bladder   brain

Which of the above organs does each of the following?
a) Controls the whole body
b) Pumps blood to all the organs
c) Stores and churns up food so that chemicals can get to work on it

d) Puts oxygen into the blood
e) Removes carbon dioxide from the blood
f) Processes and stores useful substances in the blood
g) Cleans the blood by making urine.
2 Write down *three* things that the body must take in.
3 Write down *two* ways in which the body can get rid of water.

Bones, joints, and muscles

By the end of this spread, you should be able to:
- *describe the jobs done by the skeleton*
- *describe how muscles move the body*
- *explain how muscles are controlled.*

The skeleton

Your body is supported by a framework of rigid bones called a *skeleton*. This has several important jobs to do:

Support The skeleton allows you to stand upright on the ground. It also supports vital organs inside your body.

Protection The skeleton protects many organs:

The *skull* protects the brain. The *ribs* form a cage which protects the heart and lungs. The *vertebral column* (backbone) protects the spinal cord.

Movement Many parts of the skeleton are jointed so that you can move bits of your body. The movements are made by muscles fixed to the skeleton.

Some joints just allow small movements. For example, your back can bend a little because the vertebrae have *cartilage* (gristle) discs sandwiched between them. The discs also absorb jolts.

Bone contains living cells, surrounded by hard minerals for strength. The minerals have calcium in them. Bone is also reinforced by tough *collagen* fibres which give it even more strength.

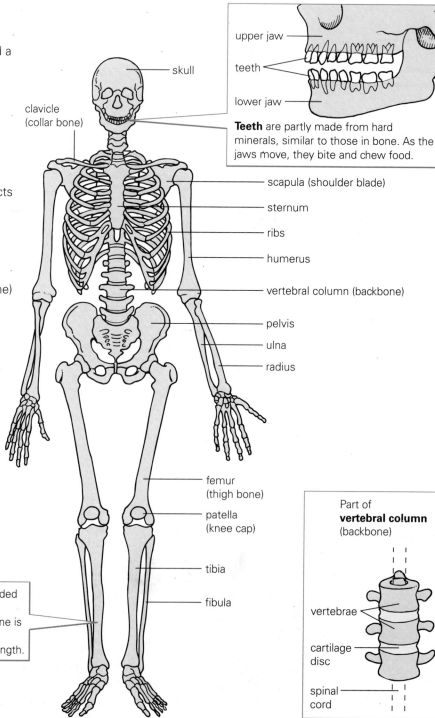

upper jaw

teeth

lower jaw

Teeth are partly made from hard minerals, similar to those in bone. As the jaws move, they bite and chew food.

skull

clavicle (collar bone)

scapula (shoulder blade)

sternum

ribs

humerus

vertebral column (backbone)

pelvis

ulna

radius

femur (thigh bone)

patella (knee cap)

tibia

fibula

Part of **vertebral column** (backbone)

vertebrae

cartilage disc

spinal cord

Joints and muscles

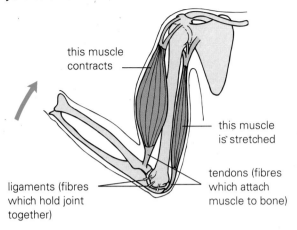

Raising arm

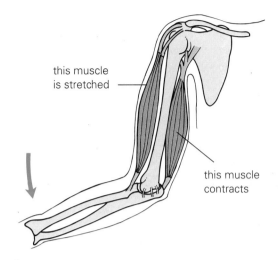

Lowering arm

Many joints are like hinges or swivels. The joints in your arms are like this. Muscles move joints by contracting (getting shorter). However, a muscle cannot lengthen itself. It has to be pulled back to its original shape. That is why muscles are often arranged in **antagonistic pairs**. One muscle pulls the joint one way, the other pulls it back.

Controlling muscles

Your muscles are controlled by the **central nervous system** (the brain and spinal cord). This is linked to all parts of the body by nerves. Signals called **nerve impulses** travel along these nerves. The central nervous system use them to sense what is happening and control your actions. For example, if you see a wasp on your hand, your eyes send signals to your brain. This sends signals to muscles, making them contract so that your hand moves.

Signals sent to the central nervous system come from **sensor cells**. The table below shows some of the things these cells respond to:

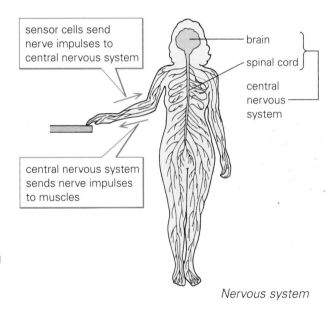

Nervous system

Sensors cells in...	respond to...
eyes	light
ears	sound
nose	chemicals in air
tongue	chemicals in food
skin	touch, pressure, heat, pain

1 Which parts of the human body are protected by **a)** the skull **b)** the ribs **c)** the vertebral column?
2 The skeleton protects many organs. Give *two* other jobs done by the skeleton.
3 Give *two* reasons why cartilage discs are needed between the vertebrae in the 'backbone'.
4 **a)** What substance is needed to make the hard minerals in bones and teeth?
   b) What else gives bone its strength?
5 What are **a)** tendons **b)** ligaments?
6 **a)** Why do muscles have to work in pairs?
   b) What are these pairs called?

Food for the body

By the end of this spread, you should be able to:
- describes the foods needed for a balanced diet
- describe what happens to food in the body.

Food is a mixture of the useful substances shown on the opposite page: carbohydrates, fats, proteins, minerals, vitamins, fibre, and water. A *balanced* diet gives you the right amounts of *all* of these.

The gut

When you swallow food, it moves down a long tube called the **gut**. This runs from the mouth to the anus. Two important things happen to food as it passes along the gut:

Food is digested This means that it is changed into a simpler, liquid form. The chemicals that do this are called **enzymes**.

Digestion mainly takes place in the stomach and small intestine. But it begins in the mouth. As you chew, an enzyme called **amylase** in your saliva starts to break down any starch into liquid glucose.

Digested food is absorbed into the blood Once food is liquid, it can pass into the blood. This mainly happens in the small intestine. Its walls are lined with tiny blood vessels which carry the food away.

Undigested matter passes into the large intestine. Here most of its water is reabsorbed by the body. This leaves a semi-solid waste (faeces) which comes out of the anus when you go to the toilet.

Like most other substances, food is made up of molecules (see Spread 3.03). During digestion, large molecules are broken down into smaller, simpler ones

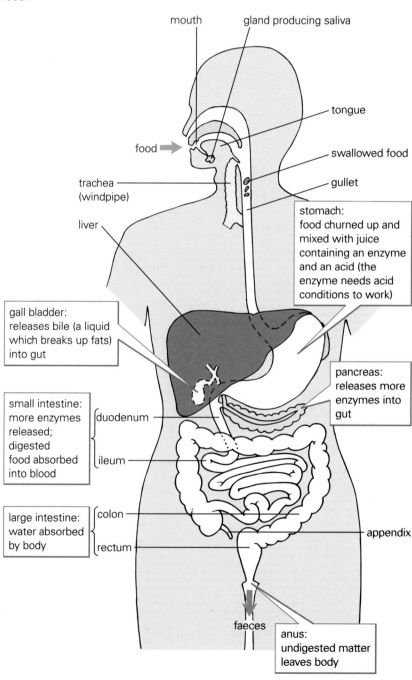

mouth

gland producing saliva

tongue

food

swallowed food

trachea (windpipe)

gullet

stomach: food churned up and mixed with juice containing an enzyme and an acid (the enzyme needs acid conditions to work)

liver

gall bladder: releases bile (a liquid which breaks up fats) into gut

pancreas: releases more enzymes into gut

small intestine: more enzymes released; digested food absorbed into blood

duodenum

ileum

large intestine: water absorbed by body

colon

rectum

appendix

faeces

anus: undigested matter leaves body

Carbohydrates
These supply about 50% of your energy.
The body breaks down sugars and starches into simple sugars like glucose. Some may also be converted into fat for storage.

Sugars in...
jams, cakes, sweets, glucose, sweet fruit
Starches in...
potatoes, rice, bread, flour

Fats (including oils)
These supply about 40% of your energy.
Fats are rich in energy. They can be stored by the body as a reserve supply of food.

Butter, margarine, vegetable oil, lard, meat, cheese

Proteins
Needed for growth and for replacing dead cells.
The body breaks down proteins into amino acids, which it can use to build new body tissues.

Meat, eggs, fish, milk, cheese, bread

Minerals
Small amounts of minerals are needed for some body tissues and for some of the body's chemical reactions.

Calcium (for making bones and teeth) in cheese, milk, vegetables
Iron (for making blood) in liver, eggs, bread
Sodium (for muscle movements) in salt

Vitamins
Small amounts of vitamins are needed to speed up some of the body's chemical reactions.

Vitamin A in margarine, butter, liver, carrots, green vegetables, fish oil
Vitamin B$_1$ in yeast, bread, meat, potatoes, milk
Vitamin B$_2$ in milk, liver, eggs, cheese
Vitamin C in blackcurrants, green vegetables, oranges
Vitamin D from margarine, eggs, fish oil

Fibre
This is the cellulose from plants. You cannot digest it, but it provides bulk. It helps food pass through the system more easily

Vegetables, cereals, bread

Water
You need about a litre of water every day – more if it is hot or you are very active

Drinks, fruit and other food with water in

---

1 a) During digestion, what do *enzymes* do?
  b) What happens to food after it has been digested?
  c) What happens to undigested food?
2 Why does the body need **a)** proteins **b)** calcium?
  Name some foods which can suppy a) and b).
3 The body cannot digest fibre (cellulose). Why is it still important in our diet?
4 *carbohydrates   fats   proteins*
  minerals   vitamins   fibre   water
  Which of the above
  a) are the body's main sources of energy?
  b) are in each of the foods on the right? Present your answers in the form of a table.

eggs

cheese

milk

bread

The lungs and breathing

By the end of this spread, you should be able to:
- describe how the lungs work
- name the gases exchanged in the lungs
- explain why smoking is bad for you.

KEY WORDS

lungs   alveoli   oxygen   carbon dioxide
gas exchange   aerobic respiration   cilia

The lungs

The cells of your body use up oxygen, as explained on the right. At the same time, they make carbon dioxide and water. Blood carries oxygen (and food) to the cells and takes carbon dioxide, water, and other waste products away. The job of the lungs is to put oxygen into the blood and remove the unwanted carbon dioxide (and some of the water).

The lungs are two spongy bags of tissue. They are filled with millions of tiny air spaces, called **alveoli**. These have very thin walls, and are surrounded by a network of blood capillaries. Oxygen in the air can seep through these walls and into the blood. At the same time, carbon dioxide (and some water) can seep from the blood into the air.

Respiration

Respiration is the chemical process by which you get energy from your food (see Spread 2.02). Your main 'fuel' is glucose sugar, produced when food is digested. In the cells of your body, the glucose is usually combined with oxygen. And, as energy is released, carbon dioxide and water are made:

glucose + oxygen → carbon dioxide + water + *energy*

Respiration using oxygen is called **aerobic respiration**. Breathing makes it possible. Carbon dioxide and water are its waste products.

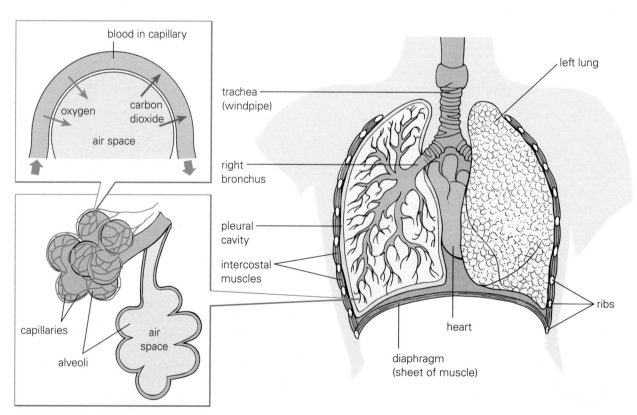

Breathing

As you breathe in and out, your lungs get bigger and smaller (see right). Some of the old air in your lungs is replaced by new, and the **exchange** of oxygen and carbon dioxide takes place.

When you are exercising, you 'burn up' food more quickly. So you must take in oxygen – and get rid of carbon dioxide – more quickly. That is why you have to breathe faster.

Smoking

Tobacco smoke contains harmful chemicals which can irritate or destroy lung tissue or cause cancer. If you smoke, you are at risk of the following:

Cancer Most of the people who die of lung cancer are smokers.

Heart disease Smokers are much more likely to suffer from heart disease than non-smokers.

Emphysema Lung tissue is destroyed, so breathing becomes more and more difficult.

Bronchitis Air passages inside the lungs become inflamed and mucus collects in them. Tiny hairs called **cilia** should break up and clear the mucus, but tobacco smoke stops them working properly.

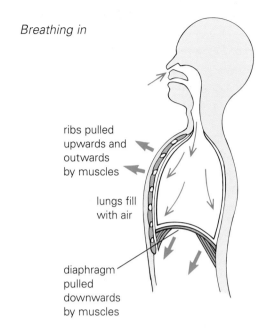

Breathing in

ribs pulled upwards and outwards by muscles

lungs fill with air

diaphragm pulled downwards by muscles

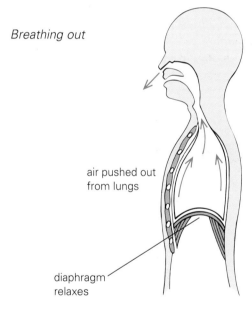

Breathing out

air pushed out from lungs

diaphragm relaxes

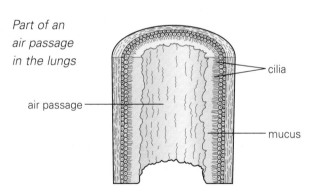

Part of an air passage in the lungs

cilia

air passage

mucus

---

1 In the lungs:
   a) what substance is taken into the body?
   b) what substances are removed from the body?
2 In the lungs, there are tiny air spaces called alveoli.
   a) Why are alveoli surrounded by blood capillaries?
   b) Why do alveoli have very thin walls?

3 In the cells of your body
   a) what substance is usually combined with oxygen in order to release energy?
   b) what are the waste products of aerobic respiration?
4 Why do you have to breathe faster when you are running?
5 Give *two* reasons why a heavy smoker might find it difficult to breathe when running.

2.08 Making human life

By the end of this spread, you should be able to:
- *explain how a sperm and an ovum combine*
- *explain the meaning of ovulation, menstruation, menstrual cycle, and fertilization.*

KEY WORDS

sperm   ovum   ovulation   ovary   uterus
menstruation   menstrual cycle   fertilization

A baby grows from a tiny cell in its mother. This cell is formed when a **sperm** from the father combines with an **ovum** (egg) inside the mother. A sperm combining with an ovum is called **fertilization**.

Puberty is the start of the time when a girl can become a mother and a boy can become a father. It often happens around the age of 12 to 14, but it is quite normal for it to be later than this. Girls usually reach puberty before boys. At puberty, girls start their periods. They also develops breasts which, later, if they have a baby, will produce milk. Boys produce sperms for the first time. Their voices go deeper and they grow more facial and body hair.

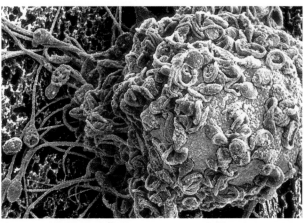

Sperms cluster around an ovum: magnification ×250

The female sex system

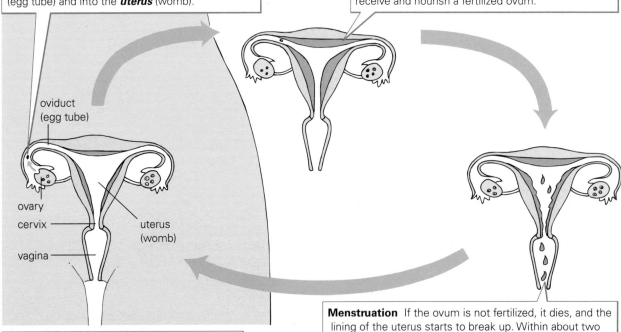

Ovulation About every 28 days, a woman releases an ovum from one of her **ovaries**. This is called **ovulation**. The tiny ovum moves down the **oviduct** (egg tube) and into the **uterus** (womb).

Lining growth Near the time of ovulation, the lining of the uterus thickens, and a network of blood capillaries grows in it. The uterus is now ready to receive and nourish a fertilized ovum.

oviduct (egg tube)

ovary

cervix

uterus (womb)

vagina

The 28-day cycle of ovulation, lining growth, and menstruation is called the **menstrual cycle**.

Menstruation If the ovum is not fertilized, it dies, and the lining of the uterus starts to break up. Within about two weeks, the woman has her **period**: blood and dead cells pass out through the vagina. This is called **menstruation**.

The male sex system

Sperms are made in a man's **testicles**. Before they leave his body, they are mixed with a liquid produced by glands. The mixture, called **semen**, leaves the penis through the same tube as urine.

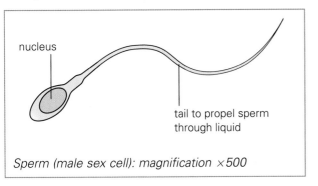

nucleus

tail to propel sperm through liquid

Sperm (male sex cell): magnification ×500

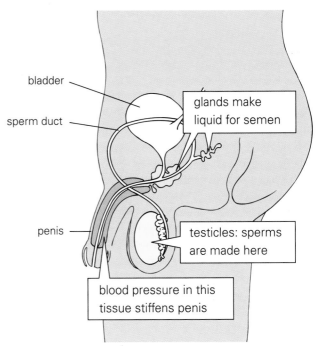

bladder

glands make liquid for semen

sperm duct

penis

testicles: sperms are made here

blood pressure in this tissue stiffens penis

How fertilization happens

When a man and woman have sex, the man's penis goes stiff and is placed in the woman's vagina. When the man **ejaculates**, semen is pumped from his penis. The semen contains millions of sperms. Some pass into the uterus. And some reach the oviducts, where they may meet an ovum. Only one sperm can fertilize the ovum. After fertilization, an extra 'skin' forms round the ovum to keep out other sperms.

Birth control

If parents want a small family, they may decide to use **contraception** (birth control). Here are some of the methods available to them:

The condom is a thin rubber cover which fits over the man's penis to trap sperms. It is more reliable if used with a **spermicide** (a cream with chemicals to kill sperms).

The diaphragm (cap) is a rubber-covered ring which is put over the woman's cervix. It too stops sperms reaching the uterus. Like a condom, it is best used with a spermicide.

The pill must be swallowed daily by the woman. It contains chemicals which stop the ovaries releasing ova (eggs). The method is very reliable, but may increase the risk of heart, liver, or breast disease in some people.

The natural method The woman does tests to find out when ovulation is close and does not have sex near that time. This method can be used by people who think that other kinds of birth control are wrong.

1 Explain what each of the following means:
   ovum   ovulation   menstrual cycle
2 About how often is an ovum released?
3 If it is not fertilized after it has been released, what happens to it?
4 What must happen to an ovum for it to be fertilized?
5 After an ovum has been fertilized, how does it stop other sperms entering?
6 Where are sperms produced?
7 Some methods of contraception are called *barrier* methods because they stop sperms reaching the uterus. Which of the methods described on this page are barrier methods?

Growing to be born

By the end of this spread, you should be able to:
- describe how a fertilized ovum becomes an embryo and then a fetus, and is kept alive in the uterus
- describe how a baby is born.

Actual sizes

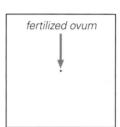

fertilized ovum

Embryo

...at 4 weeks

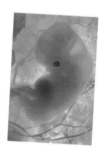

...at 7 weeks

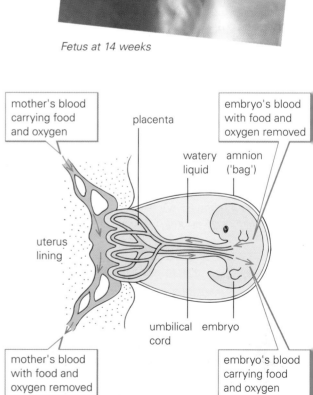

Fetus at 14 weeks

From egg to embryo

When a sperm fertilizes an ovum, the two nuclei combine to form a single nucleus. This has a full set of chemical instructions from the father and the mother to 'build' a baby by cell division.

The fertilized ovum divides over and over again as it passes down the oviduct (egg tube) and into the uterus. As more and more cells are produced, they form a tiny **embryo**. This sinks into to the thick lining of the uterus. The embryo now starts to develop into a baby. The woman is **pregnant**.

The growing embryo

At 6 weeks after fertilization, the embryo has a pumping heart and a brain. It lies in a 'bag' of watery liquid which protects it from jolts and bumps.

The embryo cannot eat and breath, so it must get all the substances it needs from its mother's body. It does this through an organ called the **placenta** which grows into the uterus lining. The embryo is linked to the placenta by an **umbilical cord**.

In the placenta, a thin membrane (sheet) separates the embryo's blood from the mother's. The two blood systems do not mix. But dissolved materials can pass from one to the other across the membrane.

Through the placenta, the embryo gets food and oxygen from its mother. Also, carbon dioxide and other waste products are taken away.

mother's blood carrying food and oxygen

placenta

embryo's blood with food and oxygen removed

watery liquid

amnion ('bag')

uterus lining

umbilical cord   embryo

mother's blood with food and oxygen removed

embryo's blood carrying food and oxygen

Birth

At 8 weeks, the embryo is beginning to look like a tiny baby. It is now called a **fetus**. At about 40 weeks (9 months), the birth takes place.

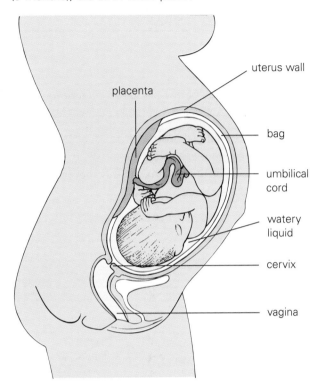

A few days before birth, the baby normally turns so that its head is by the **cervix** (the uterus entrance). As birth approaches, muscles in the wall of the uterus begin to make rhythmic contractions and the cervix starts to open. When the opening is wide enough, the baby's head passes into the vagina. At about this time, the 'bag' bursts and the watery liquid runs out.

1 Why must an ovum be fertilized before it can develop into a baby?
2 How is an unborn baby protected from jolts and bumps?
3 Explain what these are: *placenta*, *umbilical cord*.
4 How does an unborn baby get its food and oxygen?
5 How does an unborn baby get rid of its waste products?
6 How does the position of an unborn baby change a few days before birth? Why?
7 Why is it important that a pregnant mother does not drink alcohol or smoke?

Powerful contractions push the baby from the uterus and out of the mother. Shortly after the birth, more contractions push out the placenta (the 'afterbirth').

The baby gives a loud cry as its lungs fill with air for the first time. From now on, it must take in its own oxygen and food. Soon after birth, the umbilical cord is clipped and cut. Later, the remains of the cord will shrivel away to leave the navel ('belly button').

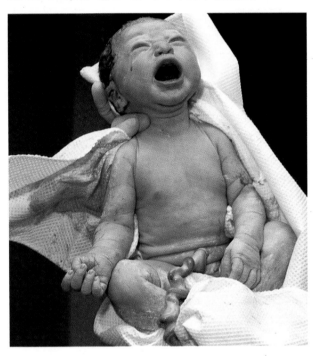

A healthy baby

Care of a baby must start long before it is born. There are many things which can threaten the health of an unborn child:

Smoking Pregnant mothers who smoke tend to have smaller babies than non-smokers. Babies born underweight have more of a struggle for survival.

Alcohol If a pregnant mother drinks alcohol, this can affect the development of her baby. Also, the baby may be premature (born too early).

AIDS Some diseases can be passed from a mother to her unborn baby. AIDS is one example.

German measles (rubella) If a mother catches German measles during the first twelve of pregnancy, it can cause deafness, blindness, and heart disease in the baby. That is why girls are given injections to stop them catching German measles later.

Microbes and health

By the end of this spread, you should be able to:
- *explain how microbes cause and spread disease*
- *describe some of the body's defences against disease.*

Microbes

Microbes are tiny living things which can only be seen with a microscope. There are billions in air, soil, and water, and in our bodies. Some do useful jobs, but some are harmful. Harmful microbes are called **germs**. Most diseases are caused by germs.

There are three main types of microbe:

Bacteria are living cells. If the conditions are right, they can multiply very rapidly by cell division. If harmful bacteria invade the body, they attack tissues or release poisons. They are the cause of sore throats as well as more serious diseases such as whooping cough, cholera, and typhoid.

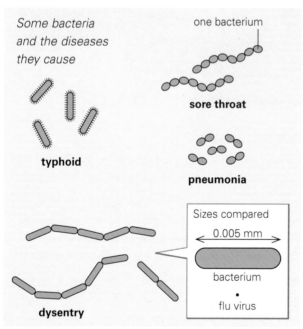

Some bacteria and the diseases they cause

one bacterium

sore throat

typhoid

pneumonia

Sizes compared

0.005 mm

bacterium

•
flu virus

dysentry

Viruses are much smaller than bacteria. They can invade living cells, multiply inside them, and upset the way they work. They are responsible for diseases such as flu, chicken-pox, and colds.

Fungi include moulds such as those which grow on old bread. Some skin diseases are caused by fungi, for example: athelete's foot and ringworm.

Spreading germs

Diseases caused by germs are called **infections**. Here are some of the ways in which they can spread:

Droplets in the air When you cough or sneeze, droplets of moisture are sprayed into the air. They carry germs which are breathed in by other people. Colds and flu are spread in this way.

Contact Some diseases can be picked up by touching an infected person. Measles is one example.

Animals Insects can leave germs on food. Blood-sucking insects such as mosquitoes put germs in the blood when they bite. Malaria is spread in this way, by one type of mosquito.

Contaminated food Sewage is full of germs. If it gets into the water supply, food and drink may be affected. Also, people may contaminate food if they have dirty hands which are covered with germs.

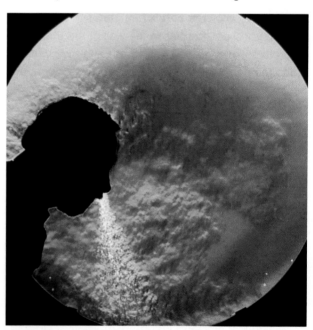

A violent sneeze. To take this photograph, a special technique was used to show air disturbances as different shades of colour.

Fighting disease

Your skin stops some germs from entering the body. However your body has an **immune system** for fighting any invaders which do get in. Its 'soldiers' are in your blood: they are **white blood cells**. Some digest germs. Others make chemicals called **antibodies** which kill germs.

Different antibodies are needed for different germs. But fortunately your immune system has a memory. Once it has made antibodies of one type, it can produce lots more of them if the same germs invade again. Once you have had, say, chicken-pox, you are unlikely to get it again. You have become **immune** to the disease. Unfortunately it is almost impossible to become immune to flu and colds. The germs keep changing, and there are many different types.

The body can be given extra help to fight disease:

Antibiotics are medicines which kill bacteria. However, they have no effect on viruses.

Vaccines contain dead or harmless germs similar to harmful ones. They are often given by injection. They make your immune system produce antibodies so that your defences are ready if the real disease attacks.

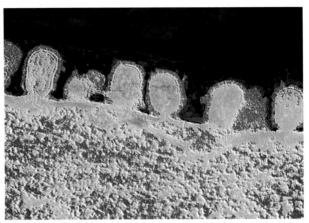

False colour photograph of flu viruses leaving an infected cell: magnification ×25000

Healthy living

To help you stay healthy, you need to eat sensibly, take plenty of exercise, and avoid health risks:

Poor diet Without enough fruit and vegetables, your body may run short of vitamins. Too little fibre can cause constipation and bowel disease. Too much fat makes you overweight and can lead to heart disease.

Smoking Smoking causes heart attacks, blocked arteries, lung cancer, and breathing difficulties.

Alcohol Years of heavy drinking can damage the liver, heart, and stomach.

Drugs Drugs make people feel excited or relaxed. But some are addictive: the body becomes dependent upon them. Many addicts die before they are 30.

Solvents Sniffing solvents is very dangerous. The vapours damage the lungs and brain.

AIDS

AIDS stands for **Acquired Immune Deficiency Syndrome**. It is a disease caused by a virus known as **HIV**. People with the virus are **HIV positive**. However, it may be many years before the full disease develops. There are treatments to slow its progress, but no known cure.

The HIV virus attacks white blood cells, so the immune system stops working. AIDS sufferers lose their defence against even mild diseases. Minor illnesses can kill them.

There are only three ways in which AIDS can be passed from one person to another:

- by sexual contact
- by blood-to-blood contact
- from an infected mother to her unborn child.

If a man wears a condom while having sex, this reduces the chances of the HIV virus passing between him and his partner.

---

1 Give *three* ways in which germs can be passed from one person to another.
2 Germs include *viruses* and *bacteria*
   Which of these
   a) are small enough to invade cells?
   b) can often be killed by antibiotics?
3 a) If you are *immune* to a disease, what does this mean?
   b) If you have been injected with a *vaccine*, why does this make you immune?
4 List some of the things you should do (or *not* do) if you want to stay as healthy as possible.

2.11 The variety of life

By the end of this spread, you should be able to:
- explain that all living things on Earth are related
- explain how living things can be put into groups.

Classifying living things

Scientists think that all living things on Earth are related. To show how closely they are related, they put them into groups with similar features. This is called **classifying**. They start by grouping them into **kingdoms**, as shown on the opposite page.

In the animal kingdom, animals with backbones are called **vertebrates**. There are five main groups. Their features are given in the table on the right.

Species

A **species** is the smallest group of living things. Members of the same species are so much alike that males and females can mate and produce young like themselves. Humans are a species, so are robins, guinea pigs, and common meadow buttercups. There are well over a million different species on Earth.

Group	Features
Fish *Examples* shark, herring, cod	Scales, fins Live in water Gills for breathing Lay eggs Varying body temperature
Amphibians *Examples* newt, toad, frog	Moist skin Live in water and on land Adults have lungs for breathing Lay eggs, usually in water Varying body temperature
Reptiles *Examples* crocodile, tortoise, lizard	Dry scales Most live on land Lungs for breathing Lay eggs Varying body temperature
Birds *Examples* robin, penguin, blackbird	Feathers Lungs for breathing Lay eggs Steady body temperature
Mammals *Examples* cat, mouse, human, whale	Hairy skin Lungs for breathing Young mostly born alive rather than in eggs Mothers make milk for young Steady body temperature

1 In the table below, the tick shows that most mammals are born alive, rather than in eggs.
   a) Copy and complete the table.
   b) What feature is common to all the groups?
   c) Which groups are egg-laying?
   d) In which group are humans? Give *three* reasons for putting them in this group.

group ▸	fish	amphibians	reptiles	birds	mammals
backbone					
lungs					
scales					
feathers					
hairy skin					
egg-laying					
young born alive					✓
steady body temperature					

Members of the same species

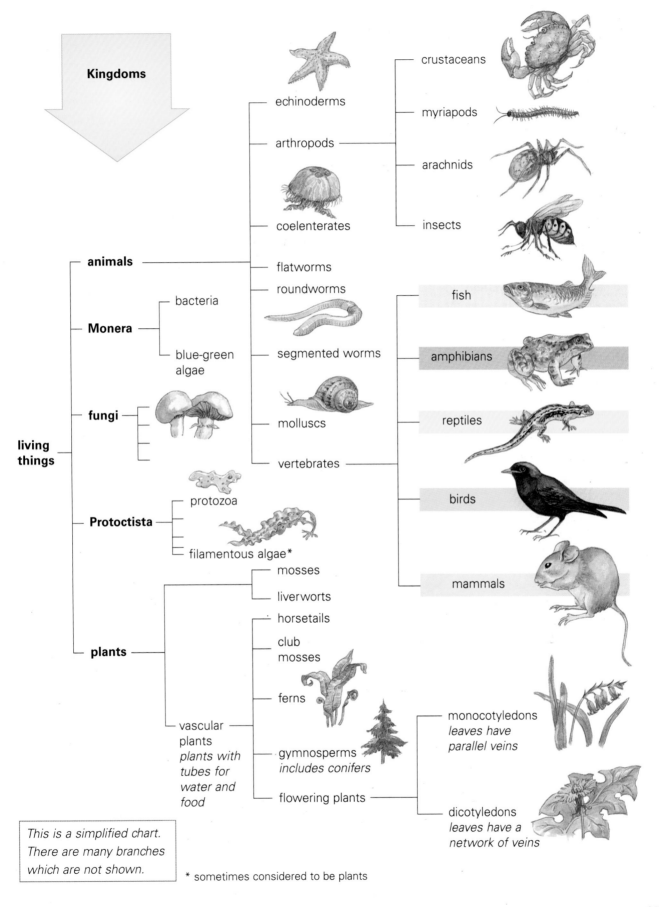

Kingdoms

- **living things**
  - **animals**
    - echinoderms
    - arthropods
      - crustaceans
      - myriapods
      - arachnids
      - insects
    - coelenterates
    - flatworms
    - roundworms
    - segmented worms
    - molluscs
    - vertebrates
      - fish
      - amphibians
      - reptiles
      - birds
      - mammals
  - **Monera**
    - bacteria
    - blue-green algae
  - **fungi**
  - **Protoctista**
    - protozoa
    - filamentous algae*
  - **plants**
    - mosses
    - liverworts
    - vascular plants
      plants with tubes for water and food
      - horsetails
      - club mosses
      - ferns
      - gymnosperms *includes conifers*
      - flowering plants
        - monocotyledons *leaves have parallel veins*
        - dicotyledons *leaves have a network of veins*

This is a simplified chart. There are many branches which are not shown.

* sometimes considered to be plants

37

2.12 The same but different

By the end of this spread, you should be able to:
- describe how living things show variation
- describe how characteristics can depend on genes and on the environment
- give some uses of selective breeding.

Variation

Your different features are called your **characteristics**. Some, like eye colour, are easy to see. Others, like your blood group, are not so obvious. No two people are exactly alike. Characteristics like height, weight, and hair colour show **variation**. 'Identical twins' are more alike than most, but even they are not *exactly* alike.

Inherited...or not?

Many of your characteristics are **inherited**: they were passed on to you by your parents. But some are affected by how you live. They depend on your **environment** (living conditions and surroundings).

All living things show variation, not just humans.

Tim and Jim are 'identical twins'. They inherited the same features from their parents: for example, their mother's black hair. But Tim and Jim are not *exactly* alike. Jim has bigger muscles because he trains in the gym. He did not inherit his bigger muscles, and they will not be passed on to his children.

Genes

A huge set of chemical instructions is needed to build a human body. Nearly every cell in your body has them. They are stored in **chromosomes** in the nucleus. Chromosomes contain a complicated chemical called **DNA** whose atoms are arranged so that they form a code. Small sections of DNA are called **genes**. You have more than 50 000 genes. Each one carries the coded instructions for a different characteristic. Other animals and plants also have chromosomes, DNA, and genes.

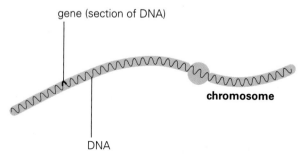

gene (section of DNA)

chromosome

DNA

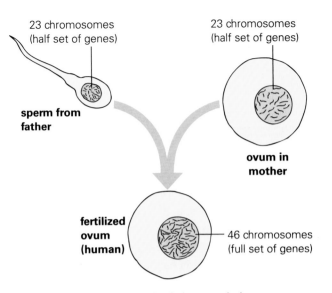

23 chromosomes (half set of genes)

sperm from father

23 chromosomes (half set of genes)

ovum in mother

fertilized ovum (human)

46 chromosomes (full set of genes)

Genes control your inherited characteristics:

You grew from a single cell, formed when a sperm from your father combined with an ovum in your mother. Sex cells (sperms and ovum) are different from other cells: they only have *half* the number of chromosomes. So people get half their genes from their mother and half from their father. But which genes come from each parent is a matter of chance. That is partly why there is so much variation.

Selective breeding

People often try to breed animals with special characteristics: for example, sheep with plenty of wool, or horses that can run fast.

Selectively bred for speed

To produce characteristics like this, people select the animals which will be mated. This is called **selective breeding**. The idea is that the offspring ('babies') may inherit the best features of both parents. But chance still affects the result. If two champion racehorses mate, their offspring will not necessarily be a champion.

Selective breeding is also used with plants. For example, one variety of wheat may grow faster than another, or be more resistant to disease. By controlling how the wheat is pollinated, scientists can breed varieties with the characteristics they want.

Genetic modification

Selective breeding can take many years. To produce useful characteristics more quickly, scientists can remove genes from one animal or plant and put them into the developing cells of another. The result is a **genetically modified** animal or plant.

Using genetic modification, scientists can produce plants that are resistant to weedkillers or pests. However, there are concerns that plants like this might harm wildlife or be difficult to control. Also, although genetically-modified (GM) food should be as safe to eat as other food, many people want more evidence before they try it.

---

1 Look at the photograph of the dogs on the opposite page. Give *three* characteristics that show variation.
2 *gene   chromosome   sperm   ovum*
   a) Which of the above carries information about one inherited characteristic?
   b) Which of the above have only half the number of genes of most other cells?
3 Give *two* examples of selective breeding.
4 Copy the table below. Decide where you think ticks should go and put them in (they can be in both columns).

characteristic	depends on genes	depends on environment
eye colour		
skin colour		
body weight		

Chains and webs

By the end of this spread, you should be able to:
- explain what food chains and food webs are
- draw a pyramids of numbers for a food chain
- explain how toxic chemicals can accumulate in a food chain.

Animals and plants need food. It supplies them with energy, and the materials they need for building and repairing their body tissues.

Plants are **producers**. They produce their own food. But animals are **consumers**. They have to get their food by consuming (eating) other living things.

Animals that kill and eat other animals are called **predators**. The animals they eat are their **prey**.

A predator and its prey

Decomposers

Some microbes (bacteria and fungi) feed on the remains of dead plants and animals. They produce enzymes which make the dead things decompose (rot) into a liquid. Then they feed on the liquid. Microbes which make things rot are called **decomposers**. They are important because:
- they get rid of dead plants and animals
- they put useful chemicals back into the soil.

Food chains

A **food chain** shows how living things feed on other living things. For example, if a blackbird feeds on snails, and these feed on leaves, then the food chain looks as below. Each arrow runs from the thing being eaten to the thing that is eating it.

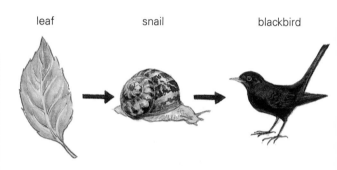

| leaf | snail | blackbird |
| producer | first consumer | second consumer |

A simple food chain

Pyramid of numbers

In a food chain, only a fraction of the energy taken in by one living thing reaches the next. So fewer and fewer living things can be fed at each stage. For example, it might take 30 000 leaves to feed 300 snails, and 300 snails to feed one blackbird. This can be shown using a **pyramid of numbers** like this:

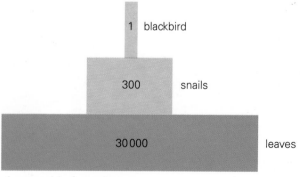

A pyramid of numbers

Food webs

Many animals eat more than one type of food. So living things can be part of several food chains. The result is a network of linked food chains called a **food web**. Here is an example:

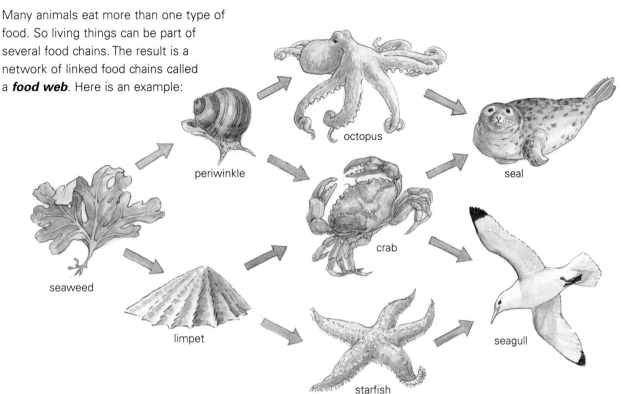

seaweed · periwinkle · octopus · seal · crab · limpet · starfish · seagull

Pollution in a food chain

If toxic (poisonous) chemicals are released into the air, water, or soil, they can enter food chains and harm or kill many things. Some chemicals get trapped in the body tissues of living things, so they accumulate (build up). Examples include some pesticides, and heavy metals such as mercury and lead. As they pass along a food chain, they become more and more concentrated. Here is an example:

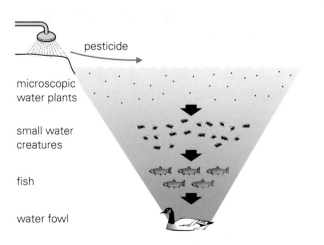

pesticide

microscopic water plants

small water creatures

fish

water fowl

1 Here are statements about some living things:

fox feeds on thrush
caterpillar feeds on cabbage
thrush feeds on caterpillar

a) Using the information above, copy and complete this food chain:

_____ → _____ → _____ → _____

Write down the names of any of the living things in the food chain which are
b) producers
c) consumers
d) predators
e) prey.
(Remember that a predator can also be prey to another animal.)

2 A frog feeds on 250 worms, which feed on 25 000 leaves. Draw the pyramid of numbers.

3 **a)** In the food web on this page, what other animals would be affected if periwinkles are poisoned by chemical waste?
b) Why do poisons become more and more concentrated as they pass along a food chain?

Adapted for living

By the end of this spread, you should be able to:
- describe some of the factors which affect living things and their environment
- explain how living things are adapted to their environment.

The place where an animal or plant lives is called its **habitat**. It is usually shared with other animals and plants. The habitat of the frog on the right is in and around a pond, where it is wet and shady. The frog needs these conditions to stop its skin drying out.

The conditions around an animal or plant are called its **environment**. They can vary from season to season, or even from hour to hour. Here are some of the factors on which they depend:

Non-living factors

Climate Some places are hotter, wetter, or windier than others.

Day and seasons It is warmer and brighter in the day than at night. It is warmer in the summer than in the winter.

Living factors

Other living things
Plants have to compete with each other for light and water. Animals feed on plants and on other animals. Often, they are in competition for a limited amount of food. Humans can drastically change the environment by clearing land, growing crops, or dumping waste.

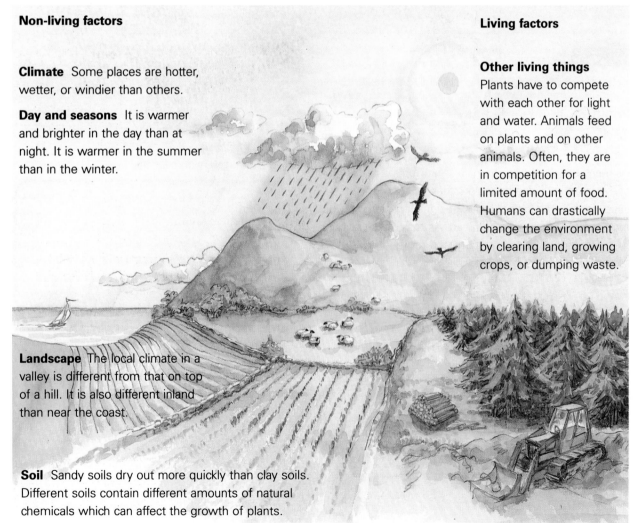

Landscape The local climate in a valley is different from that on top of a hill. It is also different inland than near the coast.

Soil Sandy soils dry out more quickly than clay soils. Different soils contain different amounts of natural chemicals which can affect the growth of plants.

Adapted for living

Over many millions of years, animals and plants have developed special features to help them cope with the conditions in which they have to live. They have become **adapted** to their environment. Here are some examples:

This hedgehog will hibernate in the winter so that it can survive when food is scarce. It will go to sleep with its life processes slowed right down.

This tree loses its leaves in the autumn. Without leaves, it needs to take up less water from the soil, so it can survive when the ground is frozen.

This owl has special features to help it catch and eat its food (see Question 3)

1 *adaptation   habitat   environment*
   Which of the above words means
   a) the conditions around an animal or plant
   b) the place where an animal or plant lives?
2 Give one way in which each of the following is adapted to survive the winter:
   a) The hedgehog, above left
   b) The tree, above right.
3 Look at the photograph on the left. Write down the special features which you think the owl has to help it
   a) hunt at night   **b)** grip small animals
   c) tear small animals apart   **d)** keep warm.
4 Give an example of
   a) how an animal's environment can change from one part of the day to another.
   b) how a plant's environment can change from one season to another.

Populations and problems

By the end of this spread, you should be able to:
- explain what limits the size of a population
- describe how human activity can affect other populations and the environment.

A group of animals or plants of the same kind is called a **population**. Animals eat plants or other animals. They also compete for food and shelter. So the size of one population affects others.

Population limit

Harvest mouse

There is a limit to the size of a population. This example shows why:

Harvest mice feed on grain. If a few mice enter a new cornfield, they have plenty of food, so they breed quickly and the population grows. But as more mice need food and shelter, survival becomes more difficult. Eventually, mice die at the same rate as new ones are born and the population stops growing. Here are some of the factors which limit it:

Predators Mice may be caught and eaten by predators such as foxes and hawks.

Food supply and shelter These may be limited.

Competitors Other animals may be competing for the same food or nesting places.

The need for protection

The world's human population is growing all the time. As it does so, it needs more crops, meat, wood, fuels, and minerals. The chart on the next page shows why many populations need protecting from the harmful effects of human activity.

Sustainable development

To develop their homes and cities, humans process natural materials like rocks (for building materials, metals, and minerals), oil (for fuels and making plastics), and wood (for buildings, furniture, and papermaking).

Some of these resources – oil and rocks for example – took millions of years to form and cannot be replaced. Others are replaceable. Softwoods (such as pine) grow quickly and, with careful planting and management, new timber can be produced at the same rate as old timber is used up. In this case, the development of the resource is **sustainable**.

Timber for buildings, furniture, and papermaking should come from sustainable forests.

Harmful effects of human activity

Human activity on Earth is causing problems for many wildlife populations, and for humans as well. Anything produced by humans which causes a harmful change to the environment is called **pollution**.

Air pollution

Carbon dioxide is the main gas given off when engines and power stations burn fuel. It isn't directly harmful to living things. But it traps the Sun's heat, and the extra amount in the atmosphere may be causing global warming.

Other waste gases Engines and power stations also produce gases which can cause acid rain, smog, and lung disease. Catalytic converters reduce the problem.

Smoke particles from factories and diesel engines damage health.

Destroying populations and habitats

Hunting and fishing Humans hunt and fish for some of their food. But killing too many animals means that not enough are left to breed. So whole populations can die out.

Cutting down forests This is done for timber or to make space for agriculture or industry. But trees supply the world with some of its oxygen and provide shelter for wildlife. Also, when trees are removed, the soil is easily eroded (worn away).

Digging up land Mining and quarrying destroy wildlife habitats and produce huge heaps of waste materials. Some contain toxic metals which can harm plants.

Building When people build houses, factories, and roads, they destroy wildlife habitats.

Growing crops When hedges are cut down to create huge fields for crops, wildlife habitats are destroyed.

Water pollution

Chemical waste is sometimes dumped into rivers or the sea.

Fertilizers and pesticides are sprayed onto fields and crops. But they can get into streams and rivers and harm wildlife.

Oil can spill from tankers. It kills sea-birds and other marine life.

Sewage is often dumped at sea. It can be a health hazard.

1 Twenty rabbits are released into a grassy area. At first, the rabbit population rises rapidly. Give *two* reasons why the population will eventually stop rising.

2 A *Using pesticides*   B *Cutting down forests*
   C *Making fields larger*
   Give *one* reason for doing each of the above. Then give *one* problem caused by each.

3 Give *one* reason why dumping rubbish, as on the left, might be harmful to **a)** animals **b)** plants.

4 Give an example of how our demand for materials might threaten an animal population.

3.01 Looking at matter

By the end of this spread, you should be able to:
- describe how the particles in a solid, liquid, and gas behave
- explain what is meant by density.

KEY WORDS

particle theory of matter   diffusion
mass   kilogram   volume
cubic metre   density   pressure

Made from particles

Materials can be solid, liquid, or gas. Scientists have come up with an idea to explain how solids, liquids, and gases behave. They call it the **particle theory of matter**:

Solids, liquids, and gases are made up of tiny particles. These are constantly on the move. They also attract each other. The attractions are strongest when the particles are close.

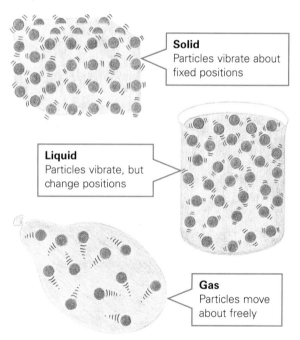

Solid
Particles vibrate about fixed positions

Liquid
Particles vibrate, but change positions

Gas
Particles move about freely

Solid The particles are held together by strong forces of attraction. The particles vibrate from side to side, but they cannot change positions.

Liquid The particles are still pulled together by forces of attraction. But strong vibrations mean that the particles have enough energy to change position and move past each other. So, the liquid can flow.

Gas The particles are spaced out, and almost free of any attractions. They move about at high speed, and quickly fill any space available.

On Earth, water exists as a solid (ice), a liquid, and a gas (water vapour in the atmosphere).

Wandering particles: diffusion

Jostled by other particles around them, some particles wander about. That is why the colours have spread on top of the trifle below. It is also why smells spread. Smells are gas particles coming from food, or perfume, or anything smelly. The wandering of particles in this way is called **diffusion**.

Mass, volume, and density

The amount of matter in something is called its mass. It can be measured in **kilograms (kg)**.

The amount of space something takes up is called its volume. It can be measured in **cubic metres** (m^3).

A block of steel has more mass in every cubic metre than a block of wood. Scientists say that steel has a greater **density** than wood.

Steel has a density of $7800 \, kg/m^3$. This means that there is 7800 kg of mass in each cubic metre. Some other density values are also shown below.

You can calculate density with this equation:

$$density = \frac{mass}{volume}$$

mass in kg
volume in m^3
density in kg/m^3

For example, if a block of coal has a mass of 3200 kg and a volume of $2 \, m^3$, its density is 3200 divided by 2, which is $1600 \, kg/m^3$.

Gases have mass. However, liquids and solids are usually much more dense than gases. For example, the lemonade in a bottle is about 750 times heavier than the air in an empty bottle.

Pressure

When you blow up a balloon, its sides are pushed out by the **pressure** of the gas inside. The particle theory explains the pressure like this. In the gas, the particles move about at high speed. As they do so, they keep colliding with the inside surface of the balloon. Each collision produces a tiny outward force. Together, millions of collisions from millions of particles produce a steady outward push.

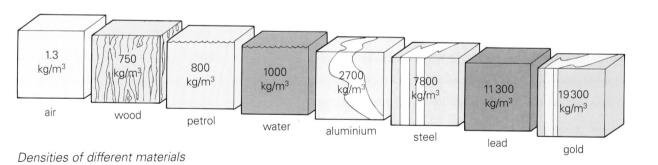

air	wood	petrol	water	aluminium	steel	lead	gold
1.3 kg/m^3	750 kg/m^3	800 kg/m^3	1000 kg/m^3	2700 kg/m^3	7800 kg/m^3	11 300 kg/m^3	19 300 kg/m^3

Densities of different materials

---

1 Say whether each of the following describes the particles in a *solid*, a *liquid*, or a *gas*:
  a) Particles well spaced out
  b) Particles close together and unable to change positions
  c) Particles close together, but able to change positions
  d) Attractions between particles very weak
  e) Particles move about freely at high speed.

2 a) How does the smell from a perfume bottle spread across a room?
  b) What is the process called?
3 Look at the chart of densities above.
  a) What is the mass of $1 \, m^3$ of water?
  b) What is the mass of $10 \, m^3$ of water?
  c) What is the mass of $10 \, m^3$ of steel?
4 Why do the gas particles in an inflated balloon cause a pressure on the sides?

Hot and cold

By the end of this spread, you should be able to:
- *describe what happens during changes of state*
- *describe what happens to a material when its temperature rises.*

Changing state

Solids, liquids, and gases are made up of tiny, moving particles (see Spread 3.01). If a material is heated, its particles speed up. For example:

If very cold ice is heated to give it more energy, its particles vibrate faster. When they gain enough energy, they can change positions, so the solid becomes a liquid. In other words, the ice melts.

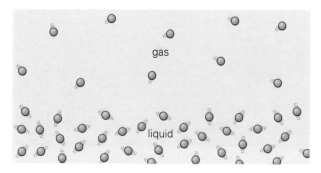

If liquid water is heated to give it more energy, its particles vibrate faster. Some move fast enough to break free of the attractions holding them together. The liquid changes into a gas (called water vapour).

A change from solid to liquid, or liquid to gas, or back again, is called a change of **state**. The diagram below shows the words used to describe the different changes of state.

The white cloud coming from a kettle is steam that has condensed to form millions of tiny droplets. The real steam (water vapour) is invisible.

Evaporation and boiling

Even cold water can evaporate – which is why wet roads and rain puddles eventually dry out. However, if water is hot enough, large bubbles of vapour form inside it and burst from its surface. This rapid type of evaporation is called **boiling**. The water vapour produced is also known as **steam**.

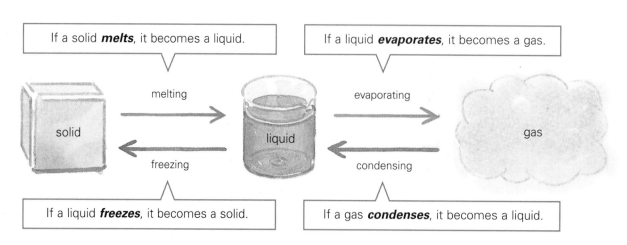

If a solid **melts**, it becomes a liquid.

melting

solid → liquid

freezing

If a liquid **freezes**, it becomes a solid.

If a liquid **evaporates**, it becomes a gas.

evaporating

liquid ← gas

condensing

If a gas **condenses**, it becomes a liquid.

Temperature

As a material gets hotter, its particles move faster. Scientists say that its **temperature** rises.

Everyday temperatures are normally measured on the **Celsius** scale (sometimes called the 'centigrade' scale.) Its unit of temperature is the **degree Celsius (°C)**. The numbers on this scale were specially chosen so that ice melts at 0°C and water boils at 100°C (under normal conditions).

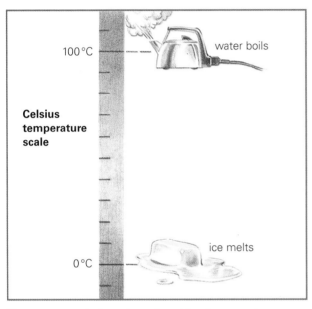

Temperatures below that of melting ice are given negative values. For example, the temperature inside a freezer might be −18°C.

As a material gets colder, its particles slow down. At −273°C, they can go no slower. This is the coldest possible temperature. It is called **absolute zero**.

The **Kelvin** scale uses absolute zero as its zero (0 K). Its 'degree' is the same size as the degree Celsius, so 0°C = 273 K and 100°C = 373 K.

Melting and boiling points

The temperature at which a solid melts is called its **melting point**. It differs from one substance to another. The **boiling point** is also different for different substances. There are some examples in the table below.

Melting and boiling points depend on pressure. The values below are for substances under the normal pressure of the Earth's atmosphere.

Substance	Melting point in °C	Boiling point in °C
hydrogen	−259	−253
oxygen	−219	−183
methane	−183	−162
mercury	−39	357
water	0	100
aluminium	660	2350
iron	1540	2760
tungsten	3387	5420

Taking a substance through its melting or boiling point does not change its mass. For example if 2 kg of water completely boils away, it forms 2 kg of steam. The particles are more spaced out, but there are just as many of them as before.

Not all solids melt when heated. For example, if wood is heated sufficiently in air, it burns and changes into a different type of material. This is an example of a chemical change (see Spread 3.06).

---

1 *condensing   evaporating   freezing   melting*

Which of the above words describes
a) a liquid changing into a gas?
b) a gas changing into a liquid?
c) a solid changing into a liquid?
d) a liquid changing into a solid?
2 If a puddle dries out, where does the water go?
3 On the Celsius scale, what is the temperature of
a) melting ice **b)** boiling water?

4 Of the eight substances given in the table above, list the one(s) you would expect to be
a) liquid, in a cold room at 5°C?
b) liquid, in a furnace at 2000°C?
c) solid, in a furnace at 2000°C?
d) solid, at the South Pole at −60°C?
e) gas, at the South Pole at −60°C?
f) liquid, in a cooling chamber at −200°C
g) gas, in a cooling chamber at −200°C

Elements, atoms, and compounds

By the end of this spread, you should be able to:
- *explain what elements, compounds, atoms, and molecules are*
- *give the two main types of elements.*

Elements

Everything is made from about 100 simple substances called **elements**. These can combine in different ways to form new substances. For example, water is made of the elements hydrogen and oxygen.

The elements can be divided into **metals** and **nonmetals**. The table below right gives some examples, along with their chemical symbols. Some of the symbols are based on old Latin names: for example, *Aurum* for gold.

Metals These are usually hard and shiny, and difficult to melt. They are good conductors of heat and electricity. A few (iron, nickel, and cobalt) are magnetic – in other words, they are attracted to magnets and can be made into magnets.

Nonmetals These are usually gases, or solids which melt easily. The solids are often brittle or powdery. Most are insulators – in other words, they are poor at letting heat or electricity through.

Carbon is unusual for a nonmetal. It exists naturally in two forms: **graphite**, which is a good conductor, and **diamond**, the hardest substance known.

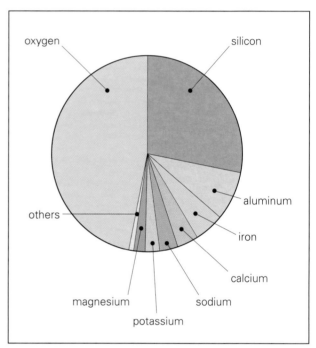

The eight most common elements in the Earth's crust (outer layer). The rocks are mainly made from oxygen and silicon.

Graphite ▶

◀ *Diamond*

Metals		Nonmetals	
Element	*Symbol*	*Element*	*Symbol*
aluminium	Al	bromine	Br
calcium	Ca	carbon	C
copper	Cu	chlorine	Cl
gold	Au	fluorine	F
iron	Fe	helium	He
lead	Pb	hydrogen	H
magnesium	Mg	iodine	I
potassium	K	nitrogen	N
silver	Ag	oxygen	O
sodium	Na	phosphorus	P
tin	Sn	silicon	Si
zinc	Zn	sulphur	S

Atoms

Elements are made up of tiny particles called **atoms**. An atom is the smallest amount of an element you can have. Atoms are far too small to see with any ordinary microscope. It would take more than a billion billion atoms to cover this full stop.

Different elements have different types of atom. Hydrogen is the lightest atom (see Spread 3.13).

Compounds

Atoms can join together to form a new substance which is quite different from the elements forming it. This new substance is called a **compound**.

Water is a compound of hydrogen and oxygen. The smallest 'bit' of water is called a **molecule** of water. It is made up of two hydrogen atoms stuck to one oxygen atom. Scientists describe it using a **chemical formula**: H_2O.

There are some examples of compounds and formulae on the right. However, not all compounds have molecules. For example, a crystal of sodium chloride (salt) is formed when millions of sodium and chlorine atoms join up in a block.

Particles of matter

According to the particle theory of matter (see Spread 3.01), solids, liquids, and gases are made up of tiny, moving particles. From their studies of elements and compounds, scientists now know what these particles are. In some substances, they are atoms; in others, they are molecules.

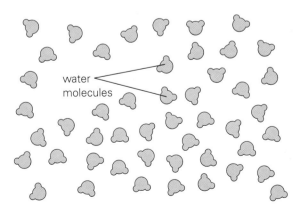

Like other substances, water is made up of tiny particles. In water, the particles are molecules.

Compound	Molecule	Formula
water		H_2O
carbon dioxide		CO_2
ammonia		NH_3
methane		CH_4
sulphuric acid		H_2SO_4

Each molecule is made up of atoms. For simplicity, the atoms have been shown as coloured spheres. But atoms do not really have a colour or exact shape.

1 What are the two main types of element?
2 Which of the eight most common elements in the Earth's crust are metals?
3 atom   molecule   compound   nonmetal
  Which of the above words means
  a) a substance formed when elements combine?
  b) the smallest possible bit of an element?
  c) the smallest possible bit of a compound such as water?
4 Write down the chemical formulae of the two compounds whose molecules are shown below.

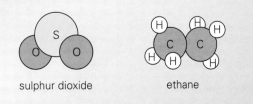

sulphur dioxide   ethane

Mixtures and solutions

By the end of this spread, you should be able to:
■ explain what mixtures, solutions, and alloys are
■ give some of the factors affecting solubility

One substance by itself is called a **pure** substance. It might be an element, such as gold, or a compound, such as water. However, very few of the substances around us are pure. For example, the bottled water in the photograph contains small amounts of other chemicals as well. If something contains at least two separate substances, it is called a **mixture**.

Solutions

If you put sand in salt, the different bits in the mixture are big enough to see. But if you put sugar in water, the sugar breaks up into particles far too small to see with a microscope. The sugar has **dissolved** in the water. The result is a mixture called a **solution**:

water
+ small amounts of
  carbon dioxide
  bicarbonates
  calcium
  chlorides
  sodium
  magnesium
  potassium
  silica
  nitrates

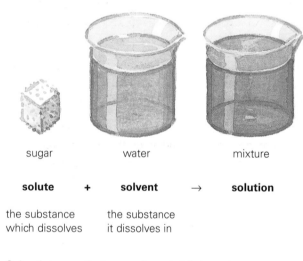

| sugar | water | mixture |

| **solute** | **+** | **solvent** | **→** | **solution** |

the substance which dissolves   the substance it dissolves in

Scientists say that sugar is **soluble** in water.

A solution containing water is called an **aqueous solution**. However, water is not the only solvent for dissolving things. Here are some others:

Solvent	Dissolves...
ethanol	Biro ink
trichloroethane	grease
propanone	nail varnish

Carbonated mineral water is a mixture. So it is not pure. But this does not mean that it is dirty. Many of the minerals in it are good for you.

Dissolved gases

Gases can also dissolve in liquids. For example, the bottled water above has carbon dioxide dissolved in it. When you take off the cap, the carbon dioxide escapes from the solution as bubbles of gas.

There is oxygen dissolved in the water around this fish. The fish uses its gills to extract it.

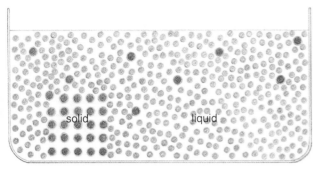

Materials are made up of tiny particles (atoms or molecules). When a solid dissolves in a liquid, its particles gradually mix with those in the liquid.

Solubility

You can only dissolve so much sugar in a hot drink. Try adding more sugar and the extra crystals will not dissolve: the solution is **saturated**. Similarly, the diagram below shows that, at 20 °C, a maximum of 20 g (grams) of copper sulphate crystals will dissolve in 100 g of water. At 20 °C, copper sulphate has a **solubility** of 20 g per 100 g of water.

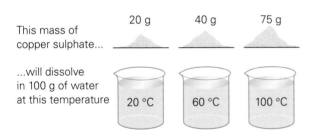

Solubility depends on the temperature Most solids dissolve more easily as the temperature rises. In other words, their solubility increases with temperature. For gases, the opposite is true: solubility decreases with temperature.

Solubility depends on the solute For example, in water, at 50 °C, potassium nitrate has *twice* the solubility of sodium chloride (common salt). In other words, you could dissolve twice as much of it.

Solubility depends on the solvent For example, in a solvent called cyclohexane, at 20 °C, iodine has *ten times* the solubility that it has in water. In other words, you could dissolve ten times as much of it.

Alloys

Brass is an alloy of copper and zinc

Metals with other substances mixed in are called **alloys**. The extra substances are added to give better properties (features). For example:

Brass is an alloy of copper (70%) and zinc (30%). It is harder than copper by itself. Also, unlike copper, it does not corrode, so it keeps its shine and colour.

Steel is an alloy of iron (99%) and carbon (1%). (Percentages vary depending on the type of steel). Steel is much stronger and harder than iron by itself.

---

1 What do scientists mean by a *pure* substance?
2 When *sodium chloride* dissolves in *water*, the result is a mixture called *brine* (salty water). Which of the substances in *italics* is
   a) the solvent   b) the solution   c) the solute?
3 a) What is an alloy?
   b) Why are metal things often manufactured from alloys rather than pure metals?
4 Look at the diagram above left.
   a) What is the solubility of copper sulphate in water at 60 °C?
   b) What happens to the solubility as the temperature rises?
   c) How much copper sulphate would dissolve in 200 g of water at 100 °C?

More mixtures and solutions

By the end of this spread, you should be able to:
- explain that air is a mixture of gases
- describe ways of separating mixtures.

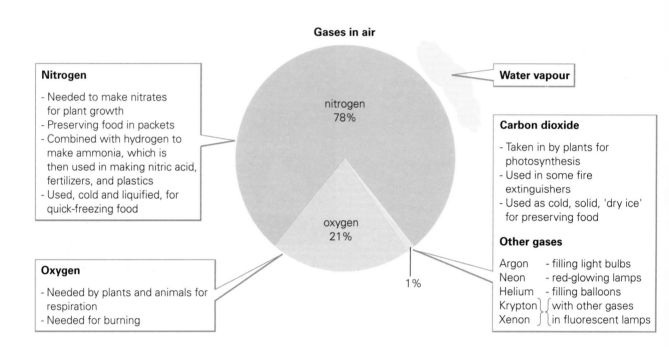

Gases in air

Nitrogen
- Needed to make nitrates for plant growth
- Preserving food in packets
- Combined with hydrogen to make ammonia, which is then used in making nitric acid, fertilizers, and plastics
- Used, cold and liquified, for quick-freezing food

Oxygen
- Needed by plants and animals for respiration
- Needed for burning

nitrogen 78%

oxygen 21%

1%

Water vapour

Carbon dioxide
- Taken in by plants for photosynthesis
- Used in some fire extinguishers
- Used as cold, solid, 'dry ice' for preserving food

Other gases
Argon   - filling light bulbs
Neon   - red-glowing lamps
Helium   - filling balloons
Krypton ⎱ with other gases
Xenon   ⎰ in fluorescent lamps

Air

Air is a mixture of gases, as shown in the chart above. Air also carries dust, smoke, exhaust fumes, and other pollutants caused by human activity.

The different gases in air have many uses, some of which are also given in the chart. Industrially, the gases are separated from each other as follows:

First, the carbon dioxide and water vapour are removed. Next, the remaining air is cooled to −200 °C, so that it turns liquid (apart from neon and helium, which are removed). Then the liquid air is slowly warmed up. The gases boil off at different temperatures and are collected separately. This process is called **fractional distillation**.

A simple form of distillation is shown on the next page. It is just one of the methods used for separating the substances in a mixture.

1 Which of the gases in air
   a) is the most plentiful?
   b) is needed by living things for respiration?
   c) is needed for burning?
   d) is used for filling balloons?
   e) can be cooled to form 'dry ice'?
2 Describe how you would separate the substances in each of the following mixtures:
   a) Sand and sugar **b)** Water and mud
   c) Water paints of different colours.
3 *tea-bag   cotton wool   bag in vacuum cleaner*
   a) Which of the above items work as filters?
   b) For each of your answers to part a, write down the substances that are being separated by the filter.

Separating mixtures

Below are some methods of separating simple mixtures in the laboratory, with examples of what they might be used for:

Filtering ▶

Example Separating sand from water.

The mixture is poured into a funnel lined with filter paper. The water passes through the paper, but the sand is stopped.

filter paper

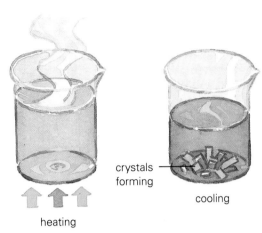

crystals forming

cooling

heating

Dissolving

Example Separating sand from salt.

The sand and salt are mixed with water and stirred. This dissolves the salt, but not the sand. The new mixture is filtered. The salty water passes through the filter paper, but the sand is stopped.

Crystallizing ▲

Example Separating copper sulphate from water.

The solution is heated gently, and some of the water evaporates. When the remaining solution is cooled, crystals of copper sulphate start to form in it.

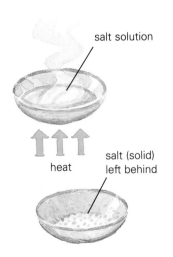

salt solution

heat

salt (solid) left behind

heat

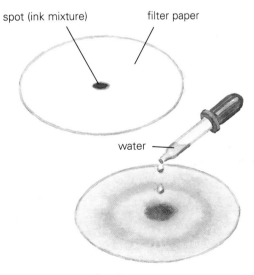

spot (ink mixture)

filter paper

water

Evaporating ▲

Example Separating salt from water.

The solution is heated gently until all the water has evaporated (turned to vapour). The salt is left behind as a solid.

Distilling ▲

Example Separating water from ink.

The mixture is boiled. The vapour, which is pure water, cools as it passes down a long tube and condenses (turns liquid).

Chromatography ▲

Example Separating inks of different colours.

A spot of ink mixture is placed at the centre of a piece of filter paper and left to dry. Water is dripped onto the spot. The ink mixture spreads through the damp paper. The different colours spread at different rates.

3.06 Chemical and physical change

By the end of this spread, you should be able to:
- explain what a chemical reaction is
- describe the differences between a chemical change and a physical change.

A chemical reaction

iron	sulphur	iron sulphide
(metal)	(yellow powder)	(black solid)

If iron filings and sulphur powder are mixed together and then heated, the two substances join to form a completely new substance, a compound called iron sulphide. This is an example of a **chemical change**. The iron has reacted with the sulphur: there has been a **chemical reaction** between the two. The reaction can be described using this **word equation**:

iron + sulphur → iron sulphide

reactants   product

When a chemical reaction takes place, as above, the atoms get rearranged so that they stick together in a different way:

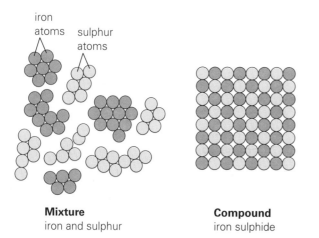

iron atoms
sulphur atoms

Mixture
iron and sulphur

Compound
iron sulphide

Signs of chemical change

If a chemical change has taken place:

One or more new substances are formed
Iron sulphide is a black solid and nothing like either iron or sulphur. For example, iron is attracted to a magnet but iron sulphide is not.

The change is usually difficult to reverse
With iron sulphide, several reactions are needed to separate the iron from the sulphur. It is not an easy process. (On the other hand, in a simple mixture of iron and sulphur, it is easy to separate the two. The bits of iron can be pulled out with a magnet.)

Energy is given out or taken in
When iron reacts with sulphur, heat is given out. (Not all reactions are like this. Some take in heat.)

These chemical reactions are giving out energy as heat and light.

Physical change

If liquid water freezes, it becomes ice. This is an example of a **physical change**. If a physical change has taken place:

No new substances are made

When water freezes, it is still the same substance, even though it is a solid.

The change is usually easy to reverse

Ice can melt to form liquid water again.

Here are two more examples of physical change:

Liquid water can change into steam. When steam condenses, it becomes liquid water again.

Salt dissolves in water. But if the water evaporates, you are left with the salt again.

No change in mass

If a substance goes through a physical change, it may look different, or change size. But its mass does not change. You still have the same number of kilograms as before.

With a chemical change, there is also no change in mass. Although a new substance is formed, the same atoms are present. They are just arranged in a different way.

1 **a)** With a mixture of iron filings and sulphur powder, how could you separate the iron from the sulphur?
   b) Why would your method not work if the iron had reacted with the sulphur?
   c) In a reaction between iron and sulphur, how does the total mass of the two compare with the mass of iron sulphide formed?

2 When *magnesium* burns, it combines with *oxygen* in the air to form *magnesium oxide*.
   a) Write a word equation for this reaction. Decide which of the substances in *italics*
   b) is a compound
   c) are the reactants
   d) is the product of the reaction.

3 Decide whether each of the following is a *chemical change* or a *physical change*, and give a reason for each answer.
   a) Hot fat going solid when cooled
   b) Sugar dissolving in water
   c) Eggs cooking, as in the photograph below.

Once eggs have been cooked, you can't change them back again.

Acids and bases

By the end of this spread, you should be able to:
- *give the main properties of acids and bases*
- *describe how litmus is affected by acids and alkalis and explain what the pH scale is used for*

Acids

There are acids in the laboratory. But there are natural acids in vinegar, sour fruits, and even in your stomach! Acids dissolved in lots of water are called **dilute** acids. The more **concentrated** an acid, the less water it is dissolved in.

Dissolved in water, acids are **corrosive** and eat into materials such as carbonates and some metals. Even without water, some concentrated acids are dangerously corrosive and should never be handled.

All acids contain the element hydrogen. In water, this becomes active and causes the acid effect. When an acid reacts with a metal, the hydrogen is given off and a compound called a **salt** is formed. You can find out more about salts and acid-metal reactions in the next spread, 3.08.

Acids that release lots of hydrogen and dissolve metals quickly are called **strong acids**. Those that release hydrogen slowly are **weak acids**. There are some examples of both types in the chart on the next page.

Some naturally-occurring acids

	contains....
lemon juice	citric acid
vinegar	ethanoic acid (acetic acid)
tea	tannic acid
sour milk	lactic acid
grapes	tartaric acid
nettle sting	methanoic acid
stomach (juices)	hydrochloric acid

Bases

Bases are the chemical 'opposites' of acids. They are compounds which react with acids and **neutralize** them (cancel out the acid effect).

Bases which dissolve in water are called **alkalis**. In other words, alkalis are soluble bases.

Alkalis can be just as corrosive as acids. Their powerful chemical action is often used in bath, sink, and oven cleaners.

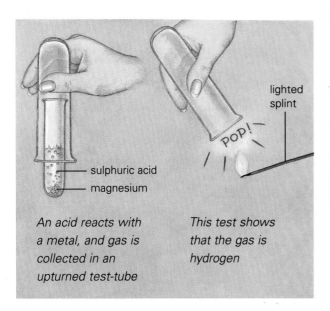

An acid reacts with a metal, and gas is collected in an upturned test-tube

This test shows that the gas is hydrogen

Alkalis, including ammonia, are used in many household cleaners.

Indicators and pH

There are some dyes which have a different colour depending on whether they are in an acidic or alkaline solution. Dyes like this are called **indicators**. Litmus is one example.

Acids turn litmus red.

Alkalis turn litmus blue.

Scientists use the **pH scale** to measure how strong or weak an acid or alkali is. The strongest acids have a pH of 1. The strongest alkalis have a pH of 14. Solutions with a pH of 7 are neither acidic nor alkaline. They are **neutral**.

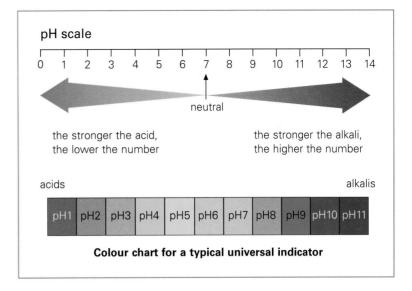

pH scale

0 1 2 3 4 5 6 7 8 9 10 11 12 13 14

neutral

the stronger the acid, the lower the number

the stronger the alkali, the higher the number

acids   alkalis

| pH1 | pH2 | pH3 | pH4 | pH5 | pH6 | pH7 | pH8 | pH9 | pH10 | pH11 |

Colour chart for a typical universal indicator

You can measure pH with **universal indicator**. This contains a mixture of dyes. It goes a different colour depending on the pH.

Strong acids	**Weak acids**	**Strong alkalis**	**Weak alkali**
hydrochloric acid	ethanoic acid	sodium hydroxide	ammonia
sulphuric acid	citric acid	potassium hydroxide	
nitric acid	carbonic acid	calcium hydroxide	

Properties of acids (in solution)

- They have a sour taste (like vinegar)
  Note: you must never taste laboratory acids
- They turn litmus red
- They react with most metals
- They react with carbonates
- They have pH numbers less than 7

Properties of alkalis (in solution)

- They feel soapy
  Note: it is dangerous to touch laboratory alkalis
- They turn litmus blue
- They react with acids and neutralize them (cancel out their acid effect)
- They have pH numbers greater than 7

---

1. What is the difference between each of these?
   a) A *concentrated* acid and a *dilute* acid.
   b) A *strong* acid and a *weak* acid.
2. What element is found in all acids?
3. Someone drops some zinc into sulphuric acid and finds that a gas is given off.
   a) How would you collect the gas?
   b) What gas is it?
   c) How could you tell that it was this gas by experiment?
4. What colour does litmus turn
   a) in an acid   b) in an alkali?
5. Someone puts some universal indicator paper into vinegar. The pH is 3. What does this tell you about the vinegar?
6. Someone puts some universal indicator paper onto wet soap. The pH is 8. What does this tell you about the soap?
7. What would you expect the pH of pure water to be?

3.08 More acids and bases

By the end of this spread, you should be able to:
- *give some examples of neutralization*
- *describe the products of acid-metal and acid-carbonate reactions*

KEY WORDS

acid base alkali salt
neutralization carbonate

Neutralization

When a base neutralizes an acid, a solution containing a salt is formed. For example:

hydrochloric + sodium   → sodium   + water
acid   hydroxide   chloride

In this case:

| acid | + | base | → | salt | + | water |

This process is called **neutralization**. Here are some practical examples. (Remember: if a base dissolves in water, it is called an *alkali*.)

- Sugar in your mouth produces acids which rot your teeth. Toothpaste is alkaline, so it neutralizes these acids.

- Acid in your stomach sometimes becomes a bit too concentrated. Indigestion tablets reduce the acidity. They contain an alkali, such as sodium hydrogencarbonate ('bicarb').

- Most plants grow best in soil that is nearly neutral. If, for example, the soil is too acidic, farmers can adjust the pH by adding lime or chalk to reduce the acidity.

- Bee stings are acidic. They can be neutralized by rubbing in calamine lotion, which contains zinc carbonate. Wasp stings are alkaline. They can be neutralized by vinegar (acetic acid).

- Nitram, the fertilizer ammonium nitrate, is made by neutralizing nitric acid with ammonia.

More salts

When people talk about 'salt', they usually mean common salt, as put on food. But there are hundreds of different salts. All can be produced by acid-base reactions. Some occur naturally. For example common salt comes from the ground or the sea. There are some examples of salts in the table.

When a bee stings you, it injects an acidic liquid into your skin. To stop the pain, the liquid needs to be neutralized.

Salt	Examples of use
sodium chloride (common salt)	flavouring food, treating icy roads
ammonium nitrate (Nitram)	fertilizer
potassium nitrate (saltpetre)	making gunpowder, fertilizer
magnesium sulphate (Epsom salts)	medicine
sodium sulphate	making glass
barium sulphate	making paint

The acid-metal and acid-carbonate reactions described on the next page produce salts. But in each case, the products also include a gas.

Acid-metal reactions

Most metals react with acids. For example, if magnesium is put into sulphuric acid, this reaction takes place:

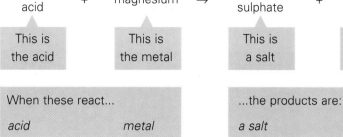

sulphuric acid	+	magnesium	→	magnesium sulphate	+	hydrogen
This is the acid		This is the metal		This is a salt		This gas is given off

When these react...		...the products are:	
acid	*metal*	*a salt*	*hydrogen*

dilute sulphuric acid

magnesium

For more about the metals which react with acids, see Spread 3.10.

Acid-carbonate reactions

Carbonates react with acids. For example, if limestone (calcium carbonate) is put into hydrochloric acid, this reaction takes place:

hydrochloric acid	+	calcium carbonate	→	calcium chloride	+	water	+	carbon dioxide
This is the acid		This is the carbonate		This is a salt		This is also made		This gas is given off

When these react...		...the products are:		
acid	*carbonate*	*a salt*	*water*	*carbon dioxide*

dilute hydrochloric acid

calcium carbonate

Rain is naturally slightly acid and eats into carbonate rocks such as limestone and chalk (see Spread 3.14). Some pollutants from factories and power stations make rain even more acidic.

One effect of acid rain

1 *carbon dioxide   salt   water   hydrogen*
   Which of the above are made
   a) when an acid reacts with a metal?
   b) when an acid reacts with a carbonate?
2 When sulphuric acid reacts with copper oxide, copper sulphate and water are made.
   a) Write a word equation for this reaction.
   In this reaction:
   b) which substance is a base?
   c) which substance is a salt?
3 Give a practical example of
   a) an alkali being used to neutralize something acidic
   b) an acid being used to neutralize something alkaline.

Burning

By the end of this spread, you should be able to:
- describe the products of burning
- give the conditions needed for burning
- describe some of the environmental problems caused by burning fuels.

Combustion

Combustion is another word for burning. It happens when substances react with oxygen in the air, and gives out energy as heat and light.

When an element burns, it becomes **oxidized**. The product of the reaction is an **oxide**. For example:

sulphur + oxygen → sulphur dioxide

magnesium + oxygen → magnesium oxide

Extra weight If you burn magnesium ribbon in a crucible and trap the ash, the ash weighs more than the magnesium because of the added oxygen:

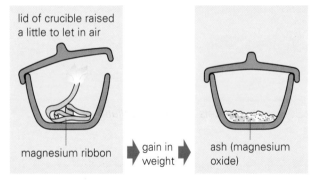

lid of crucible raised a little to let in air

magnesium ribbon → gain in weight → ash (magnesium oxide)

Burning fuels

Natural gas is mainly methane, a compound of hydrogen and carbon. When methane burns in oxygen, the atoms become rearranged to form molecules of carbon dioxide and water, as shown below:

Most fuels contain atoms of hydrogen and carbon, and produce carbon dioxide and water when they burn. Examples include petrol, diesel, kerosene (jet fuel), coal, wood, and ethanol (alcohol).

Respiration is a kind of 'slow combustion' without any flames (see Spread 2.02). Our body cells use it to get energy from glucose:

glucose + oxygen → carbon dioxide + water

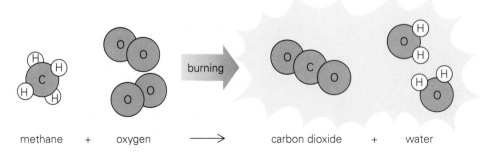

methane   +   oxygen   ⟶   carbon dioxide   +   water

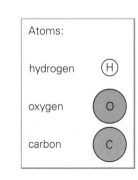

Atoms:

hydrogen   Ⓗ

oxygen   🔵

carbon   Ⓒ

Testing for oxygen

Fuels burn more fiercely in pure oxygen than in air. You can use this fact to test for oxygen. If a smouldering wooden splint is put into a jar containing oxygen, the splint will burst into flames.

Testing for carbon dioxide

Carbon dioxide turns a liquid called **limewater** milky. You can use this fact to tell that there is carbon dioxide in the air you breathe out. Just gently blow through limewater with a drinking straw and watch what happens.

Fire!

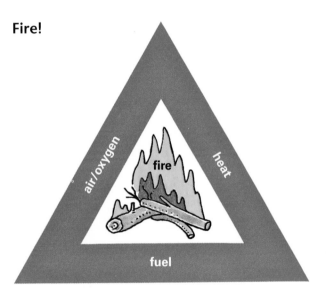

The **combustion triangle** above shows the three things needed for burning. Removing any of them stops the burning. So firefighters have three ways of putting out a fire:

● **Cutting off the fuel**, for example, by turning off the gas at the mains.

● **Cutting off the air supply** by using fire blankets, sand, foam, or carbon dioxide gas from an extinguisher.

● **Getting rid of the heat**, for example, by cooling things down with water.

Note: water is not safe for some fires. It conducts electricity and can give people shocks. And if it is thrown on burning fat or oil, this can splatter and spread.

Fossil fuels and the environment

Coal, oil, and natural gas are called **fossil fuels**: they were formed from the remains of plants and tiny sea creatures which lived many millions of years ago. We use these fuels in our homes, factories, and vehicles – for example, petrol, diesel, and jet fuel are all extracted from crude oil.

Burning fossil fuels releases huge amounts of energy. But it damages the environment by polluting the atmosphere – see **Air pollution** in Spread 2.15.

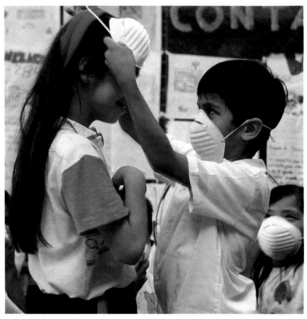

Burning fossil fuels causes air pollution

1   *oxygen   methane   carbon dioxide*
   Which of the above gases
   a) is needed for burning?
   b) is used to put out fires?
   c) makes a smouldering splint burst into flames?
   d) turns limewater milky?
   e) is made when a fuel such as petrol burns?
   f) is made when your body 'burns up' food?
2   Explain each of the following:
   a) When magnesium ribbon burns, its ash weighs more than the ribbon.
   b) Completely covering burning wood with a fire-proof blanket will stop it burning.
3   Give *two* examples of environmental damage caused by burning fossil fuels. (You may need to look at Spread 2.15 to answer this.)

Metals and reactivity

By the end of this spread, you should be able to:
■ describe how metals react with oxygen, water, and
  acids, and what the products are
■ explain what the reactivity series is.

Some metals are more **reactive** than others. They combine more readily with other substances to form compounds.

Reacting with oxygen

The chart below gives examples of how different metals react if heated and put into a gas jar containing pure oxygen. If a reaction takes place, the product is an oxide.

Metal	Reaction with oxygen	Product
sodium	burns very easily after only gentle heating	sodium peroxide (pale yellow powder)
magnesium	burns easily with brilliant white flame	magnesium oxide (white powder)
iron	only burns if in the form of a powder or wire-wool	iron oxide (black powder)
copper	does not burn, but black substance forms on surface	copper oxide (black powder)
gold	no reaction, even with strong heating	–

Reacting with water

The chart below gives examples of how different metals react with water. If a reaction takes place, hydrogen gas is given off.

Metal	Reaction with water	Products	
sodium	reacts violently and catches fire	hydrogen (gas)	+ sodium hydroxide (in solution)
magnesium	reacts slowly	hydrogen (gas)	+ magnesium oxide (solid)
iron	no reaction in cold water, reacts with hot steam	hydrogen (gas)	+ iron oxide (solid)
copper	no reaction	–	
gold	no reaction	–	

Safety
With care, the experiment below can be done in a school laboratory. However, experiments with sodium are too dangerous for you to do yourself.

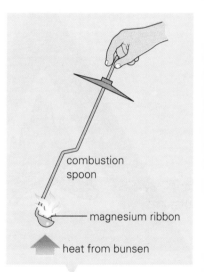

combustion spoon

magnesium ribbon

heat from bunsen

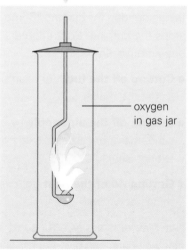

oxygen in gas jar

Testing magnesium to see how it reacts with oxygen

Reacting with acid

The chart on the right gives examples of how different metals react with dilute hydrochloric acid. If a reaction takes place, hydrogen gas is given off. Also, the reaction is much faster than with water by itself.

For more on acid-metal reactions and salts, see Spread 3.08.

Metal	Reaction with dilute hydrochloric acid	Products
magnesium	reacts very quickly	hydrogen + magnesium chloride (gas) (salt, in solution)
iron	reacts steadily	hydrogen + iron chloride (gas) (salt, in solution)
copper	no reaction	–
gold	no reaction	–

The reactivity series

From results like those described, scientists have produced a 'league table' to show how reactive different metals are. It is called the **reactivity series**. There is a short version below (hydrogen has also been included, although it is not a metal.)

most reactive

potassium (K)

sodium (Na)

calcium (Ca)

magnesium (Mg)

} these metals react with acids

aluminium (Al)

zinc (Zn)

iron (Fe)

lead (Pb)

hydrogen (H)

copper (Cu)

silver (Ag)

least reactive   gold (Au)

Mining iron ore

Finding metals

Metals are found in rocks. The rocks containing them are called **ores**. They are mined (dug from the ground) so that the metal can be extracted.

Reactive metals readily form compounds, so they are not found as pure metals. For example iron has to be extracted from a brown, rusty compound called **haematite**. On the other hand, gold, which is very unreactive, is found as tiny pieces of metal.

1 Look at the tables showing how metals react with oxygen, water, and acid. In these tables:
   a) is magnesium always more reactive than iron?
   b) is iron always more reactive than copper?
   c) which metal is always unreactive?
   d) what gas is given off when a metal reacts with water or acid?
   e) if an oxide is produced, but nothing else, what has the metal reacted with?
2 Explain why, during mining
   a) aluminium is never found as pieces of metal
   b) gold is always found as pieces of metal.

More metals and reactivity

By the end of this spread, you should be able to:
- explain what happens in a displacement reaction
- explain how metals may compete for oxygen
- explain why some metals corrode

Some metals are more reactive than others. Here is a reminder of the **reactivity series**:

most reactive

least reactive

potassium
sodium
calcium
magnesium
aluminium
zinc
iron
lead
hydrogen
copper
silver
gold

Displacement reactions

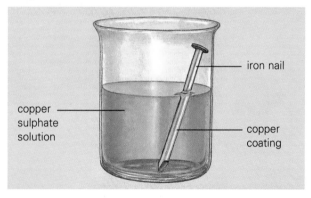

iron nail

copper sulphate solution

copper coating

If an iron nail is placed in copper sulphate solution, iron slowly dissolves, while copper is deposited on the nail as a brown coating:

iron + copper sulphate → copper + iron sulphate
(solid)   (in solution)   (solid)   (in solution)

This is an example of a **displacement reaction**. Iron is more reactive than copper, so it more readily forms compounds with other substances. In the solution, the iron and copper are competing with each other to form the sulphate. The iron wins, so it *displaces* (pushes out) the copper from the solution.

Displacing hydrogen

There is a displacement reaction whenever a metal reacts with an acid. For example:

When magnesium ribbon is dropped into hydrochloric acid, the magnesium dissolves and hydrogen gas is given off. This is why it happens:

Like all acids, hydrochloric acid contains hydrogen (see Spread 3.08). In the reactivity series on the left, magnesium is more reactive than hydrogen, so it displaces hydrogen from the solution. The hydrogen bubbles off as a gas.

The other metals above hydrogen in the series also react with acids by displacing hydrogen.

Competing for oxygen

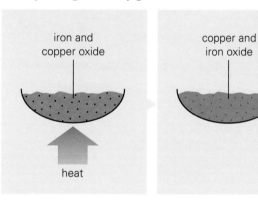

iron and copper oxide

copper and iron oxide

heat

If a mixture of powdered iron and copper oxide is heated, as above, a reaction takes place, and the mixture starts to glow as heat is released by the reaction. The products of the reaction are iron oxide and copper:

iron + copper oxide → copper + iron oxide

In this case, the iron and copper are competing for the oxygen. But iron is more reactive than copper, so it wins the competition and takes the oxygen away from the copper. Scientifically speaking, the iron is being **oxidized**, while the copper oxide is being **reduced**. The iron is an **oxidizing agent**.

Corrosion

The surface of a metal may be attacked by other substances around it. The effect is called **corrosion**. Iron corrodes by slowly reacting with oxygen and water vapour in the air. The product is the brown, flaky substance we call **rust**. It is a form of iron oxide. Steel, which is mainly iron, can also go rusty.

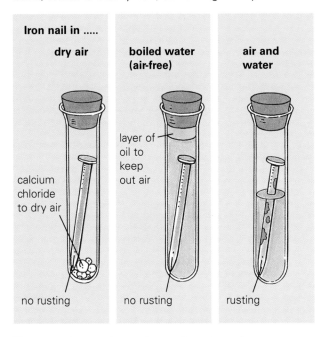

Iron nail in .....

dry air	boiled water (air-free)	air and water

calcium chloride to dry air

layer of oil to keep out air

no rusting | no rusting | rusting

Iron slowly reacts with oxygen and water vapour in the air to form rust.

The experiment above shows that air *and* water are needed for rusting. Dry air alone has no effect. Nor does water, if all air has been removed by boiling.

To stop rusting, iron and steel can be coated with paint, grease, plastic, or another metal, to keep out air and water. (Stainless steel does not rust, but is too expensive for many jobs).

Gold is very unreactive and does not corrode.

1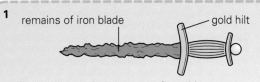

   remains of iron blade   gold hilt

   The old sword above was found in an underground chamber.
   a) Why has much of the blade disappeared but not the handle?
   b) If the air in the chamber had been very dry, what difference would this have made?

2 Copper wire is placed in silver nitrate solution. As the copper dissolves, the solution turns blue, and a silver coating forms on the wire.
   a) Which is more reactive, copper or silver?
   b) Why does a silver coating form on the wire?
   c) Copy and complete the following word equation to show the reaction that occurs:

   copper + silver nitrate → _____ + _____

3 Say whether a reaction will take place in each of the following cases, and give a reason for your answer.
   a) Copper placed in zinc nitrate solution.
   b) Zinc placed in dilute hydrochloric acid.
   c) Copper placed in dilute hydrochloric acid.
   d) Copper heated with zinc oxide.

Made by reactions

By the end of this spread, you should be able to:
- give examples of useful materials made by chemical reactions
- give examples of problems caused by reactions.

Most of the materials around us, and inside us, are the products of chemical reactions.

Metals from reactions

Iron and aluminium are two of our most useful metals. They come from rocks called ores, which contain oxides of the metals (see Spread 3.10). Chemical reactions are used to extract them from their oxides.

Iron	Aluminium
Ore haematite *contains* iron oxide (a compound of iron and oxygen)	**Ore** bauxite *contains* aluminium oxide (a compound of aluminium and oxygen)
Extracting the metal The ore is heated strongly in a blast furnace with coke and limestone. Chemical reactions remove the oxygen, leaving molten (melted) iron.	**Extracting the metal** An electric current is passed through molten aluminium oxide. This causes a reaction which releases the oxygen and leaves molten aluminium.

Molten iron runs from a blast furnace.

Made from oil

Oil companies get their oil from the ground. They call it **crude oil**. It is a mixture of substances. Petrol, kerosene, and diesel oil can all be separated from the mixture and used as fuels. However chemical reactions (sometimes with additional substances) can turn the compounds in oil into a whole range of plastics, including polythene, polystyrene, and PVC. There are some examples below:

Reactions in living things

Living things use chemical reactions to get energy and make new body tissue:

In your body, chemical reactions make blood, flesh, and bone out of materials in your food and drink.

Trees and other plants use chemical reactions to make wood, stems, and leaves out of carbon dioxide from the air and water from the ground. To do this, they need the energy in sunlight (see Spread 2.02).

In all living things, the reactions are started or speeded up by natural chemicals called **enzymes**.

Made by microbes

Microbes, such as bacteria and fungi, are microscopic living things. Some are harmful (see Spread 2.10), but some can be useful. All of the following drinks and foods are made by chemical reactions caused by enzymes from microbes:

Wine is made from grapes. Yeast microbes change the sugar in the grapes into alcohol and carbon dioxide gas. The process is called **fermentation**.

Beer is also made by fermentation. But the starter materials are grain and sugar, rather than grapes.

Cheese is made from milk. Microbes make the milk go sour and lumpy. The lumpy bits are changed into cheese by putting in more microbes.

Yoghurt is also made from milk. Enzymes from microbes make the milk go thick and slightly sour.

Microbes are needed to make these from milk.

Rusty, rancid, and rotten

Not all chemical reactions are useful. Rusting (see Spread 3.11) is one example of an unwanted chemical reaction. Here is another:

Fatty foods can react with oxygen in the air. When oxidized, they taste unpleasant. People say they are *rancid*. Foods such as crisps and cheese are often packed and sealed in bags filled with nitrogen to stop the fat in them becoming oxidized. (For more about nitrogen, see Spread 3.05.)

The apples below are rotting because of chemical reactions caused by microbes called **decomposers** (see Spread 2.13). These change the apples into a liquid. Rotting apples are no good to eat, but the liquid can put useful chemicals back into the soil.

As these apples rot, liquid seeps into the soil.

---

1 *wood   polythene   iron   alcohol   cheese*

Which of the above materials
a) is made from compounds in oil using chemical reactions?
b) is made from sugar using chemical reactions?
c) is extracted from its oxide using chemical reactions?
d) is made from carbon dioxide and water using chemical reactions?

2 Which of the materials in Question 1 are produced by the action of microbes?

3 a) Why do packets of crisps like the one above have nitrogen in them rather than ordinary air?
b) Give another example of an unwanted chemical reaction.

The periodic table

By the end of this spread, you should be able to:
- *explain what the periodic table is*
- *describe how elements with similar properties are grouped in the table.*

The **periodic table** is a chart showing the elements. In the simplified version below, each element is represented by its chemical symbol. There is a more detailed version on page 117. The table is made up of rows and columns. The rows are called **periods**. Some of the columns have **group** numbers.

Properties and positions

Elements can differ greatly in their **properties** (features). For example, one may be more reactive than another, or have a greater density.

In the periodic table, the elements are set out in such a way that elements in the same group (column) have similar properties. For example, the elements in Group 1 are all reactive metals of low density. The elements in Group 0 are all very unreactive gases.

Although elements in the same group have similar properties, they do not have the *same* properties. In group 7 for example, bromine (Br) is liquid at room temperature, while iodine (I) is solid.

	Element	Symbol		Element	Symbol
1	hydrogen	H	20	calcium	Ca
2	helium	He	21	scandium	Sc
3	lithium	Li	22	titanium	Ti
4	beryllium	Be	23	vanadium	V
5	boron	B	24	chromium	Cr
6	carbon	C	25	manganese	Mn
7	nitrogen	N	26	iron	Fe
8	oxygen	O	27	cobalt	Co
9	fluorine	F	28	nickel	Ni
10	neon	Ne	29	copper	Cu
11	sodium	Na	30	zinc	Zn
12	magnesium	Mg			
13	aluminium	Al	86	radon	Rn
14	silicon	Si	87	francium	Fr
15	phosphorus	P	88	radium	Ra
16	sulphur	S	89	actinium	A
17	chlorine	Cl			
18	argon	Ar	atomic number (see next page)	For other elements see page 117	
19	potassium	K			

Periodic table

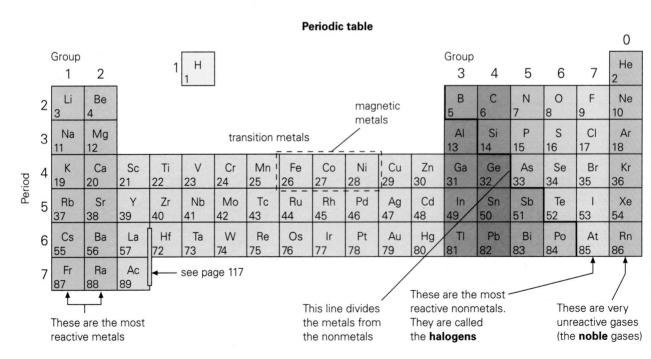

This line divides the metals from the nonmetals

These are the most reactive nonmetals. They are called **the halogens**

These are very unreactive gases (the **noble** gases)

These are the most reactive metals

transition metals

magnetic metals

see page 117

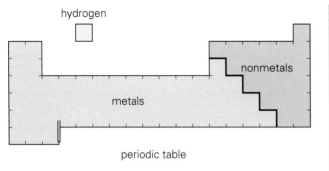

periodic table

The elements can be divided into **metals** and **nonmetals** (see Spread 3.03). Hydrogen has properties of both types, so, in the periodic table, it is usually placed on its own.

Numbering the elements

In the periodic table on the opposite page, the elements have all been numbered. Hydrogen (number 1, at the top of the table) has the lightest atoms. Of the elements shown, actinium (number 89, at the bottom of the table) has the heaviest atoms – although there are heavier elements in the more detailed version of the periodic table on page 117.

The number next to each element is called its **atomic number**. If you want to find out exactly what it means, read the panel on the right.

---

1 Decide whether each of these elements is a *metal* or a *nonmetal*:

   calcium   sulphur   argon   chromium

2 Give *two* features which the elements in Group 1 have in common.

3 Give *two* features which the elements in Group 0 have in common.

4 Name an element which you would expect to have similar properties to carbon.

5 From the information in the periodic table on the left, you can tell that iodine (I) is a very reactive nonmetal. Give as much information as you can about each of these elements:

   neon   sodium   nickel

Atoms, electrons, and properties

An **atom** is the smallest possible bit of an element. The mass of an atom is mainly concentrated in a tiny **nucleus** in the centre. Around this nucleus, there are even tinier particles called **electrons**. Each element has a different number of electrons in its atom. Hydrogen has 1 electron: its **atomic number** is 1. Actinium has 89 electrons: its atomic number is 89.

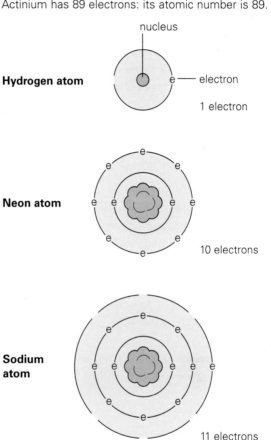

The diagrams above show atoms of three elements. Each diagram is just a convenient and simple way of representing an atom. Scientists call it a **model**. In a real atom, the electrons are not really arranged in neat circles around the nucleus.

The outer electrons of an atom are the bits that take part in chemical reactions. They make atoms stick together when compounds are formed. For example:

In a sodium atom, there is a single outer electron. This readily sticks to other atoms, so sodium is very reactive.

In a neon atom, the outer electrons form a closed 'shell'. None will readily stick to other atoms, so neon is very unreactive.

Elements in the same group have similar properties because they have similar electron arrangements.

3.14 Rocks and fragments

By the end of this spread, you should be able to:
- *explain that most rocks are a mixture of minerals*
- *describe how rocks can be weathered*
- *describe how rock fragments are recycled.*

The Earth's crust (outer layer) is made of rock. There is rock beneath the ground you walk on, and rock beneath the oceans. On cliffs and mountain peaks, the rock is exposed (out in the open). But in other areas of land, the rock is usually covered with soil.

Made from minerals

A *mineral* is any substance which occurs naturally in the Earth, usually in the form of tiny crystals.

There are many different types of rock. Most are a mixture of mineral particles. Two of the most common minerals in rock are quartz (silicon dioxide, or silica) and calcite (calcium carbonate).

In rocks, the individual crystals are called *grains*. In some cases, they are so small that you need a microscope to see them. They may be stuck together in a hard lump, or loose. For example, sand is a rock.

This piece of granite is a mixture of tiny crystals.

Weathering

Exposed rock may be weakened and broken up by the action of the weather. This is called *weathering*. The diagram below shows how it can happen:

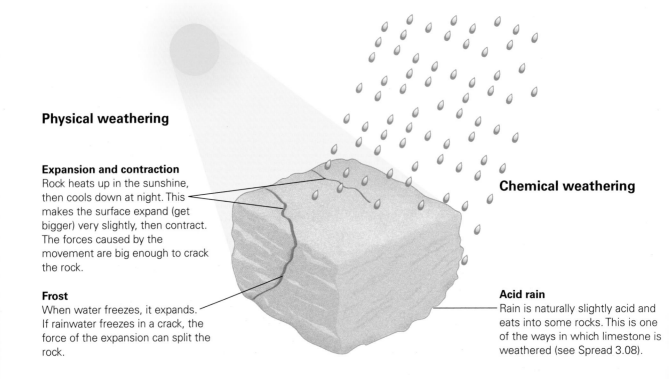

Physical weathering

Expansion and contraction
Rock heats up in the sunshine, then cools down at night. This makes the surface expand (get bigger) very slightly, then contract. The forces caused by the movement are big enough to crack the rock.

Frost
When water freezes, it expands. If rainwater freezes in a crack, the force of the expansion can split the rock.

Chemical weathering

Acid rain
Rain is naturally slightly acid and eats into some rocks. This is one of the ways in which limestone is weathered (see Spread 3.08).

Recycling rocks

Materials from rocks are used over and over again. The process can take millions of years:

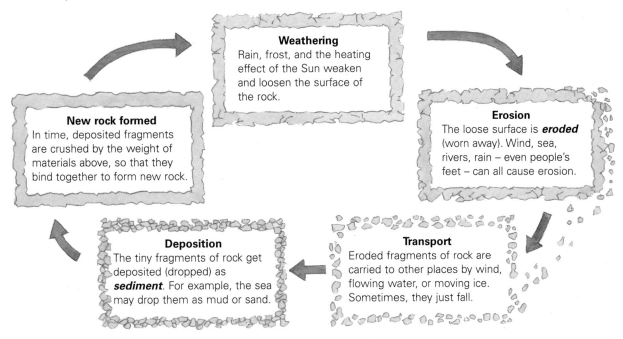

Weathering
Rain, frost, and the heating effect of the Sun weaken and loosen the surface of the rock.

New rock formed
In time, deposited fragments are crushed by the weight of materials above, so that they bind together to form new rock.

Erosion
The loose surface is *eroded* (worn away). Wind, sea, rivers, rain – even people's feet – can all cause erosion.

Deposition
The tiny fragments of rock get deposited (dropped) as *sediment*. For example, the sea may drop them as mud or sand.

Transport
Eroded fragments of rock are carried to other places by wind, flowing water, or moving ice. Sometimes, they just fall.

For more about rock forming, see the next spread.

Soil

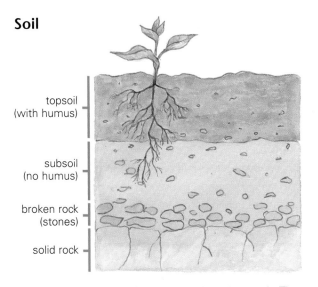

topsoil (with humus)

subsoil (no humus)

broken rock (stones)

solid rock

Soil is mainly formed from the rock underneath. The rock gets broken up by the processes described on the left. The bigger fragments are stones. The smaller ones become the soil. The top layer also contains *humus* (decayed plant and animal matter).

In some places, soil is formed from the sediment left when a sea or river retreats.

The effect of weathering and erosion

1 Give *three* ways in which the weathering of a piece of rock can happen.
2 **a)** What is meant by *erosion*?
   b) Give *three* examples of things that can cause erosion.
3 Soil often contains stones. Where do the stones come from?
4 Explain how fragments worn away from one rock can end up as part of new rock.

3.15 Forming rocks

By the end of this spread, you should be able to:
- *describe how igneous, sedimentary, and metamorphic rocks are formed*
- *describe some of the features of these rocks.*

Rocks are formed by changes happening on the Earth's surface and beneath it.

The Earth's structure

The core is mostly molten (melted) iron, though the inner core is kept solid by the great pressure there. Deep in the core, the temperature reaches 5000 °C.

The mantle is mostly solid rock made of silicates (compounds of silicon and oxygen). However, the heat and pressure keep it flexible, rather like Plasticine. Driven by heat from the core, it slowly circulates. Near the surface, any release of pressure turns it liquid. This hot, molten rock is called *magma*. Sometimes, it comes out of volcanoes as *lava*.

The crust is the Earth's thin outer layer. The continents are the thickest part (up to 90 km). They are mainly made of *granite* and 'float' like huge rafts on the denser mantle underneath. Under the oceans, the crust is thinner and mainly *basalt*.

Over many millions of years, the shape of the crust slowly changes. The continental rafts move. Rocks are worn away by erosion. Pockets of magma become exposed. And rivers and seas advance and retreat.

The Earth

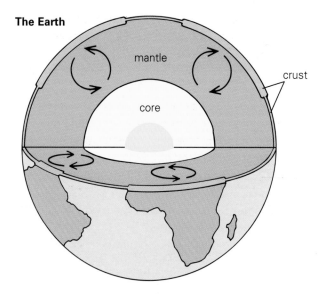

Lava (molten magma) from a volcano

Rocks can be grouped into three main types, called *igneous*, *sedimentary*, and *metamorphic*:

Igneous rocks   *Examples* granite, basalt

These are formed when molten magma cools and solidifies. If it cools *quickly*, the crystals are *small*. This happens when magma is exposed on the surface. If it cools *slowly*, the crystals have time to grow, and are *large*. This can happen to magma deep in the crust. It may take thousands of years for a large pocket of magma to cool and solidify.

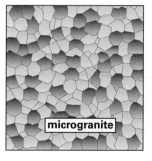

microgranite

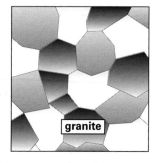

granite

This rock cooled more quickly...   ...than this

Sedimentary rocks *Examples* sandstone, limestone

This sandstone formed from fragments worn away from other rocks.

This limestone formed from the shells and skeletons of ancient, tiny sea creatures.

Sedimentary rocks are formed from layers of sediment deposited by seas, rivers, wind, or glaciers. The sediments are compressed as more and more material collects above them. Then they harden and set like concrete. This process can take millions of years. The layers of rock are called **strata**.

Most sediments are fragments of eroded rock. However, some are bits of shells and skeletons from tiny sea creatures which lived millions of years ago. Limestone, which is mainly calcium carbonate, is usually formed from bits like this. But, it can also be formed in another way:

Sea water contains dissolved calcium carbonate. When warm, shallow seas evaporate, the solid is deposited – rather like the scale in a kettle.

Metamorphic rocks *Examples* marble, slate

Deep underground, igneous and sedimentary rocks can be changed by heat or pressure or both. They become metamorphic ('changed') rock. This is usually harder than the original:

Original rock		Metamorphic rock
limestone	$\xrightarrow{\text{heat}}$	marble
shale (mudstone)	$\xrightarrow{\text{pressure}}$	slate

1 *magma   strata   lava*

Which of the above words means
a) molten rock from a volcano?
b) molten rock in the Earth's mantle?
c) layers of rock?

2 *sedimentary   igneous   metamorphic*

Which of the above rocks are formed
a) when molten magma cools and solidifies?
b) by the action of heat or pressure on existing rocks?
c) from material deposited by water or wind?

3 Why do some igneous rocks have larger crystals in them than others?

4 Why might fossils be found in limestone but not in granite?

5 The photograph below shows a piece of slate.
a) How is slate formed?
b) Why does the slate have layers in it?

Electricity on the move

By the end of this spread, you should be able to:
- explain where electricity comes from
- explain what conductors and insulators are
- describe how a simple circuit works.

What is electricity?

Electricity can power torches, toasters, and TVs. It can even light up the sky in a flash. But what is it? The answer lies in the atom:

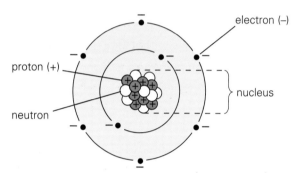

An atom has a tiny **nucleus**, made up of smaller particles (**protons** and **neutrons**). Around this are even smaller particles called **electrons**.

In an atom, there are two types of electric **charge**. Electrons have a **negative** (–) charge, protons have a **positive** (+) charge. Atoms normally have the same number of electrons as protons, so, overall, they are uncharged.

Electrons do not always stay attached to atoms. When you switch on a light, the 'electricity' in the wires is actually a flow of electrons.

A flow of electrons is called a **current**.
Put another way: a current is a flow of charge.

Conductors and insulators

Conductors are materials which let electrons flow through. In a conductor such as copper, some electrons are so loosely attached to their atoms that they are free to flow between them.

Insulators are materials which do *not* let electrons flow through. Their electrons are held tightly to atoms, and are not free to move.

Semiconductors are 'inbetween' materials. They can be treated chemically to control how much they conduct, and are used in microchips.

Conductors		Semiconductors	Insulators
Good	*Poor*	silicon	plastics
metals,	human body	germanium	e.g.
especially	water		PVC
silver	air		polystyrene
copper			Perspex
alumnium			glass
carbon			rubber

A simple circuit

An electric **cell** can make electrons move. But there must be a conducting material between its two **terminals**. Then, a chemical reaction inside the battery will push electrons out of the negative (–) terminal and round to the positive (+) terminal.

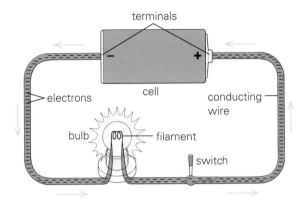

The cell above is being used to light up a bulb. The conducting path through the bulb, wires, switch, and cell is called a **circuit**. As the electrons pass through the bulb, they make a **filament** (thin wire) heat up so that it glows.

There must be a *complete* circuit for the current to flow. If the circuit is broken, the flow of electrons stops, and the bulb goes out. Turning the switch OFF breaks the circuit by separating two contacts.

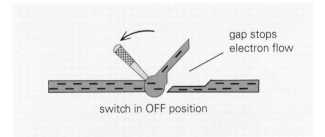

gap stops electron flow

switch in OFF position

Cells and batteries

If you want to use a computer game like the one above, or a torch, or a portable CD player, or a TV remote controller, you usually have to fit several cells in it.

A **battery** really means a collection of cells. However, people often use the word 'battery' when talking about a single cell.

Some batteries are manufactured with several cells in them. The car battery below is like this. It contains six cells:

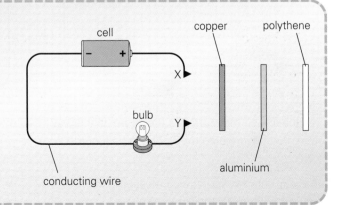

---

1 *copper   polythene   PVC   aluminium   carbon*
  Which of the above materials are
  a) conductors **b)** insulators?
2 In the circuit on the right, would you expect the bulb to light up or not? Give a reason for your answer.
3 In the circuit on the right, what would be the effect of placing the following between the contacts X and Y?
  a) a copper rod   **b)** an aluminium rod
  c) a polythene rod.

Circuits and cells

By the end of this spread, you should be able to:
■ explain how current and voltage are measured
■ describe the differences between series and parallel circuits.

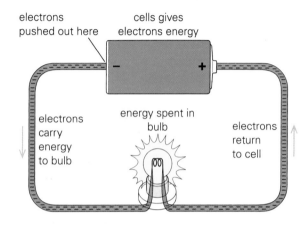

In the circuit above, the cell is *giving* the electrons energy as it pushes them out. The electrons are *spending* this energy when they flow through the bulb. The energy is given off as heat and light. (For more on energy, see Spread 4.08).

Current

Current is measured in **amperes (A)**. The higher the current, the greater the flow of electrons.

Current is measured with an **ammeter**, connected into the circuit like this:

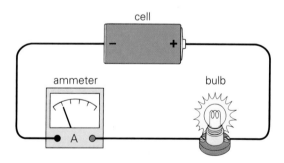

The ammeter can be connected anywhere in this circuit, because the current is the same all the way round. Putting in the ammeter doesn't affect the flow of electricity.

Small currents are sometimes measured in **milliamperes (mA)**. 1000 mA = 1 A

Voltage

Cells have a **voltage** marked on the side. It is measured in **volts (V)**. The higher the voltage, the more energy each electron is given to spend.

The voltage of a cell can be measured by connecting a **voltmeter** across its terminals:

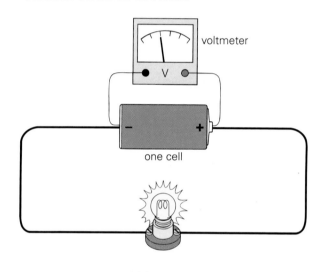

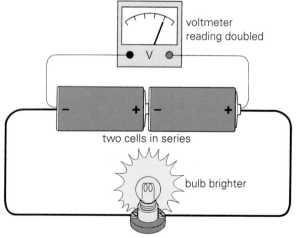

If *two* cells are connected in **series** (in a line), the total voltage is doubled. Also, the bulb is brighter because more current is pushed through it:

● The more cells in series, the higher the voltage.
● The higher the voltage, the higher the current.

Series and parallel

Here are two different ways of adding an extra bulb to the previous circuit:

Bulbs in series The bulbs glow dimly. It is more difficult for the electrons to pass through two bulbs than one, so there is less current than before.

Adding more bulbs makes them even dimmer. And if *one* bulb is removed, the circuit is broken. So *all* the bulbs go out.

Bulbs in parallel The bulbs glow brightly, because each is getting the full voltage from the cells. However, together, two bright bulbs take more current than a single one, so the cells will not last as long.

If one bulb is removed, there is still a complete circuit through the other bulb, so it keeps glowing brightly.

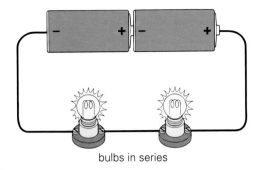
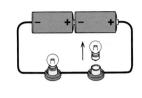
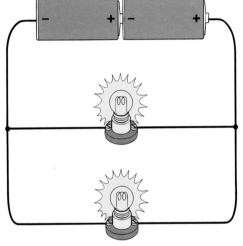

bulbs in series

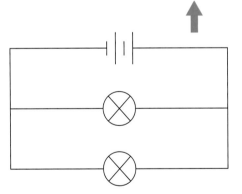
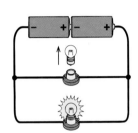

bulbs in parallel

Circuit symbols

It can take a long time to draw pictures of circuits! That is why scientists and electricians prefer to use **symbols**.

On the right, you can see the circuit with bulbs in parallel, drawn using symbols.

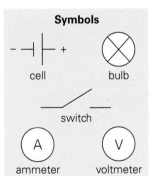

Symbols

- –| |+ +   ⊗
  cell   bulb

  ⟋ switch

  Ⓐ   Ⓥ
  ammeter   voltmeter

---

1 In the circuit on the right, what type of meter is X? What reading would you expect to see on it?

2 What type of meter is Y?

3 Redraw the circuit so that it has two cells instead of one, and Y is across both. What difference would you expect to see in
a) the brightness of the bulb   **b)** the reading on X
c) the reading on Y?

4 If an extra bulb is added to your new circuit in *series*, how will this affect **a)** the brightness **b)** the current?

5 What are the advantages of connecting the extra bulb in *parallel*?

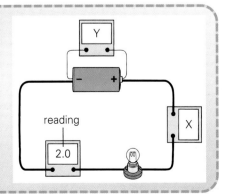

Magnets and electromagnets

By the end of this spread, you should be able to:
■ *describe the effects of magnets and electromagnets*
■ *explain some of the uses of electromagnets.*

Magnets

A few metals are **magnetic**. They are attracted to magnets and can be magnetized. The main magnetic metals are iron and steel.

The force from a magnet seems to come from two points near the ends. These are called the **north pole (N)** and the **south pole (S)** of the magnet.

When the poles of a magnet are brought close, you can feel a force between them:

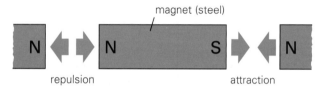

magnet (steel)

repulsion   attraction

Like poles repel. Unlike poles attract.

Magnetic fields

A magnet will push or pull on other magnets, and attract unmagnetized pieces of iron and steel nearby. Scientists say that the magnet has a **magnetic field** around it. You can use a **compass** to see the direction of the forces from this field. (A compass is a tiny magnet which is free to turn on a spindle and line up with the field.)

Electromagnets

An electric current produces a magnetic field. This effect is used in the **electromagnet** shown below.

When a current is passed through the **coil**, a magnetic field is produced. The iron **core** makes the field much stronger. The field is even stronger if
● the current is increased
● there are more turns on the coil.

When the current is switched off, the iron core *loses* its magnetism. However, a steel core would *keep* its magnetism. This idea is used to make magnets.

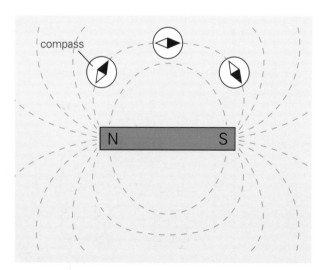

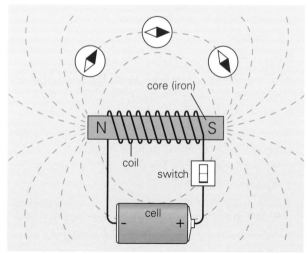

Using electromagnets

The big advantage of an electromagnet is that its pulling force can be 'switched' on and off.

The electromagnet in the photograph on the left is being used to lift (and then drop) pieces of iron and steel. It cannot lift non-magnetic metals.

Here are two more uses for electromagnets:

Magnetic metals	Non-magnetic metals	
iron	aluminium	zinc
steel	copper	brass
cobalt	tin	lead
nickel	gold	silver
	stainless steel	

Magnetic relay This is a switch operated by an electromagnet. With a relay, it is possible to use a tiny switch with thin wires to turn on the current in a much more powerful circuit – for example, a mains circuit with a big electric motor in it.

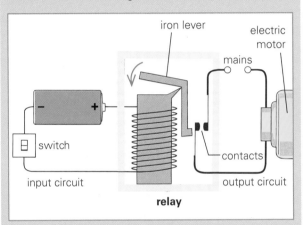

relay

How it works If you switch on the current in the input circuit, the electromagnet pulls on an iron lever. This closes two contacts in the output circuit, so a current flows through the motor.

Many relays have extra contacts which can be used if you want to switch an output circuit *off* by switching the input circuit on.

Circuit breaker This is an automatic safety switch. It cuts off the current in a circuit if this gets too high.

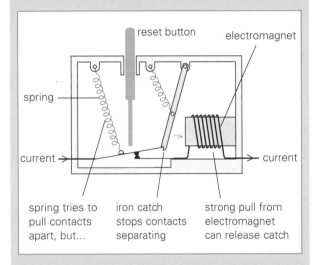

How it works The current flows through two contacts and also through an electromagnet. A spring is trying to pull the contacts apart, but there is an iron catch stopping them from opening. If the current gets too high, the pull of the electromagnet becomes strong enough to release the catch, so the contacts open.

---

1 What type of magnetic pole
   a) attracts an N-pole b) repels an S-pole?
2 How would the pulling force of an electromagnet be affected by
   a) using a coil with more turns?
   b) reducing the current through the coil?
   c) changing the iron core for a copper core?
3 a) What is the advantage of using a relay to switch on an electric motor?
   b) Describe what happens inside the relay when the switch in the input circuit is turned on.

4 In the diagram below, describe what will happen when the switch is turned ON.

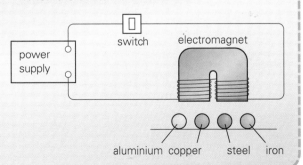

Forces

By the end of this spread, you should be able to:
- describe how forces are measured
- explain that weight is the force of gravity
- describe the effects of balanced and unbalanced forces.

A force is a push or pull. There are some examples of forces on the right and below:

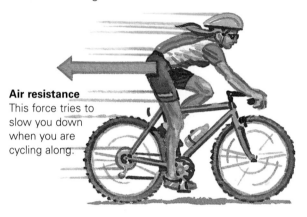

Air resistance
This force tries to slow you down when you are cycling along.

Tension This is the force in a stretched spring, string, or rope.

Weight This is the downward force of gravity (see below).

Measuring force

Force is measured in **newtons (N)**.

Below, a force is being measured with a **newtonmeter**. This has a spring inside. The greater the force, the more the spring stretches and the further the pointer moves along the scale.

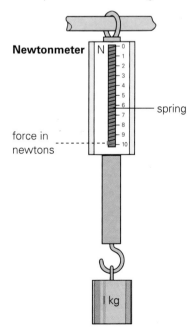

Newtonmeter

N
0
1
2
3
4
5
6
7
8
9
10

spring

force in newtons

I kg

The force of gravity

We are pulled to the Earth by the force of gravity. No one knows what causes gravity, but scientists do know that there is a gravitational attraction between *all* masses.

The gravitational force between everyday objects is far too weak to detect. It only becomes strong if one of the objects has a huge mass, like the Earth. For example, there is a gravitational pull between the Sun, Earth, Moon, and planets. For more about this, see Spread 4.18.

The force of the Earth's gravity on an object is called its **weight**. Like other forces, it is measured in newtons.

On Earth, a mass of 1 kilogram has a weight of about 10 newtons, as shown in the diagram on the left.

Balanced and unbalanced forces

A skydiver jumps from a helicopter. As she falls, there are two forces on her: *air resistance* (upwards) and her *weight* (downwards)...

gaining speed

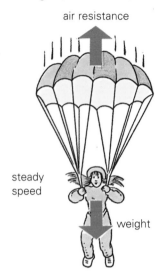

air resistance

At first, the downward force is stronger than the upward force. The forces are **unbalanced**, so the skydiver **accelerates** (gains speed).

Now, the forces are equal. They are **balanced**. Neither force wins, so she doesn't speed up or slow down. Her speed is *steady*.

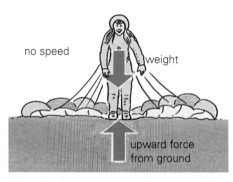

Now she is standing on the ground. The ground is compressed. It pushes upwards and supports her weight. Once again, the forces are *balanced*.

If an object has *unbalanced* forces on it, its motion will change:

Depending on the direction of the forces, the object will gain speed, lose speed, or move in a different direction.

If an object has *balanced* forces on it, its motion will *not* change:

If the object is still, it will stay still. If it is moving, it will keep moving with the same speed and direction.

1 In diagram A on the right, a ball is hanging from a piece of string. The ball weighs 6 N.
   a) What does the letter N stands for?
   b) Copy diagram A. Draw in an arrow to show the force on the ball from the string.
   c) What is the strength of this force in N?

2 In diagram B, the ball is falling through air, and has reached a steady speed.
   a) Copy diagram B. Draw in an arrow to show the force of air resistance on the ball.
   b) Is this force *more* than the weight, *less* than the weight, or *equal* to the weight?

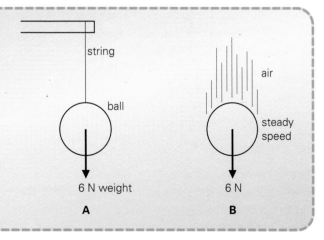

Moving and stopping

By the end of this spread, you should be able to:
- calculate speed
- describe how friction can be useful, and a nuisance, and how to reduce it.

Speed

Here is a simple method of measuring speed. You could use it to work out the speed of a cyclist:

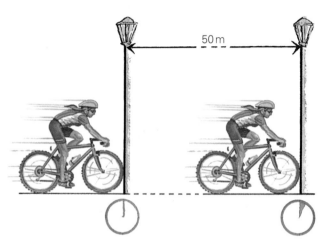

50 m

5 seconds later

Measure the distance between two points on a road, say two lamp posts. Measure the time the cyclist takes to travel between these points. Then use this equation:

$$\text{average speed} = \frac{\text{distance travelled}}{\text{time taken}}$$	distance in m time in s speed in m/s

The diagram shows that the cyclist travels 50 metres (m) in 5 seconds (s). So:

$$\text{average speed} = \frac{50}{5}$$

$$= 10 \text{ metres per second.}$$

This is written 10 m/s for short.

On most journeys, the speed changes, so the actual speed isn't always the same as the average speed. To find an actual speed, you have to find the distance travelled in the shortest time you can measure.

Friction

Friction is the force that tries to stop materials sliding past each other. There is friction between your hands when you rub them together, and friction between your shoes and the ground when you walk along. Air resistance is also a type of friction.

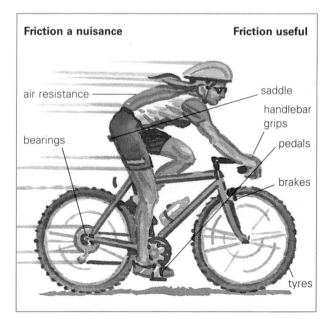

Friction a nuisance · Friction useful

air resistance · saddle · handlebar grips · bearings · pedals · brakes · tyres

Friction can be useful or it can be a nuisance. The last diagram on the opposite page gives some examples. There are some more below.

Using friction

Without friction between the tyres and the ground, you would not be able to ride a bike. It would be like riding on ice. You could not speed up, turn, or stop.

Brakes rely on friction. The wheels of a cycle are slowed by pressing rubber blocks against the rims. The wheels of a car are slowed by pressing fibre pads against metal discs attached to the wheels. But none of these brakes would be any good without friction between the tyres and the ground.

Problems with friction

Friction slows moving things and produces heat. In machinery, grease and oil reduce friction so that moving parts do not overheat and seize up. Ball bearings and roller bearings also reduce friction. Their rolling action means that a wheel does not rub against its shaft.

If a car could speed along without air resistance, it would use much less fuel. Car designers cannot get rid of air resistance, but they can give the car a streamlined shape to reduce it as much as possible. Drivers can reduce air resistance and save fuel by not driving so fast.

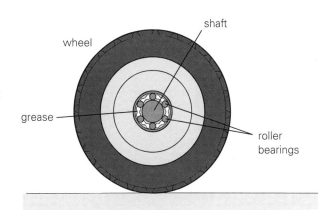

Friction slows a car down when the brakes are applied.

Reducing friction in a wheel

A car body being tested in a wind tunnel

1 Sian cycles 100 metres in 10 seconds.
   a) What is her average speed?
   b) If she keeps a steady speed, how far will she travel in 15 seconds?
   c) If she keeps a steady speed, how many seconds will she take to travel 200 metres?
2 Look at the photograph on the opposite page. What features can you see for reducing friction?
3 For a car, where is friction
   a) useful?
   b) a nuisance?
   Give *two* examples of each.
4 **a)** Give *two* ways in which the force of air resistance on a car can be reduced.
   b) What are the advantages of reducing air resistance?

4.06 Pressure

By the end of this spread, you should be able to:
■ explain what pressure is and how to calculate it
■ describe some of the effects of pressure.

Measuring pressure

You can't push your thumb into wood. But you can push a drawing pin in using the same force. This is because the force is concentrated on a much smaller area, as shown on the right. Scientists say that the **pressure** is greater.

Pressure is measured in **newtons per square metre** (**N/m²**), also called **pascals** (**Pa**). There are two examples below.

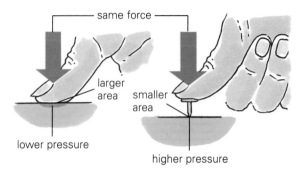

Concentrating a force increases the pressure

Pressure can be calculated with the following equation:

$$pressure = \frac{force}{area}$$

force in N
area in m²
pressure in Pa

For example, in the bottom diagram on the left, a force of 2000 N is pressing on an area of 2 m². Using the equation to calculate the pressure:

$$pressure = \frac{2000}{2} = 1000\,Pa$$

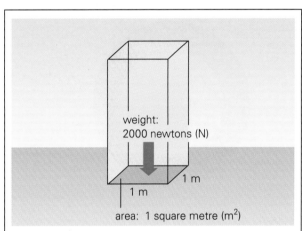

weight: 2000 newtons (N)

1 m
1 m

area: 1 square metre (m²)

This block weighs 2000 newtons. So there is force of 2000 newtons pressing on 1 square metre of ground.

The pressure under the block is 2000 newtons per square metre, or 2000 pascals.

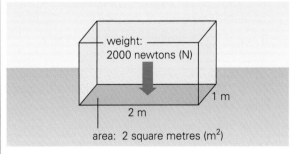

weight: 2000 newtons (N)

1 m
2 m

area: 2 square metres (m²)

This block also weighs 2000 newtons. But it is pressing on 2 square metres of ground. So there is a force of 1000 newtons on *each square metre* of ground.

The pressure under the block is 1000 newtons per square metre, or 1000 pascals.

Tyre pressure gauges are sometimes marked in 'psi' (pounds per square inch). The pressure in this tyre is 50 psi, which is about 350 000 pascals.

Pressures low and high

Spreading the force over a *large area* gives...	*Concentrating* the force on a *small area* gives...
low pressure	**high pressure**

This ski spreads the skier's weight so that the foot does not sink into soft snow.

When the studs on this boot are pressed down, they sink into the ground to give good grip.

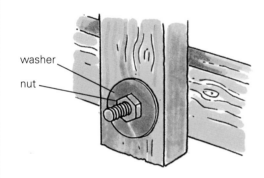

washer

nut

When the nut is tightened, the washer spreads the force, so that the nut does not sink into the wood.

A sharp blade concentrates the force from your hand so that cutting is easy.

1 N m^2 N/m^2 Pa

  a) What do each of the above stand for in words?

  b) Which of the above are units of pressure?

2 Use your ideas about pressure to explain each of the following:

  a) it is easier to walk on soft sand if you have flat shoes rather than shoes with small heels.

  b) it is easier to cut through something with a knife if the knife has a very sharp blade.

3 The block on the right weighs 1200 newtons.

  a) What is the area under the block?

  b) What is the pressure under the block?

  c) If the block is tipped over so that it is resting on its side, what will the pressure under it then be?

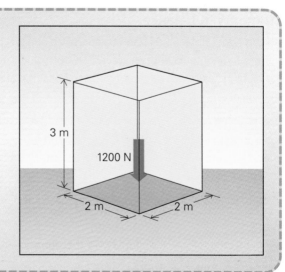

3 m

1200 N

2 m   2 m

4.07 Turning forces

By the end of this spread, you should be able to:
- *calculate the turning effect of a force*
- *explain why some things balance.*

Moments

Forces can have a turning effect.

Below, someone is using a spanner to turn a bolt. With a longer spanner, they could use the same force to produce an even greater turning effect.

The strength of a turning effect is called a **moment**. It can be calculated with this equation:

moment	=	force	×	distance from turning point
in Nm		in N		in m

The distance is the *shortest* distance from the turning point to the line of the force. A turning point is also known as a **pivot**.

Forces can have a turning effect

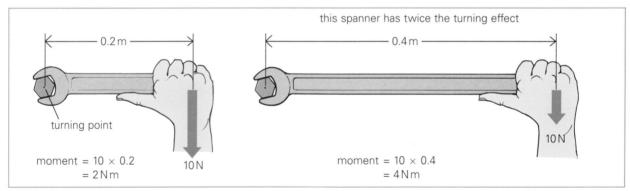

this spanner has twice the turning effect

0.2 m

turning point

moment = 10 × 0.2
       = 2 Nm

10 N

0.4 m

moment = 10 × 0.4
       = 4 Nm

10 N

Moments in balance

On the right, a plank has been balanced on a log. Different weights have been placed on both sides of the plank. They have been arranged so that the plank still balances.

One weight has a turning effect to the left. The other has a turning effect to the right. The two turning effects are equal, and cancel each other out. That is why the ruler balances.

In other words, if something balances:

moment	=	moment
turning to the left		turning to the right

This is an example of the **law of moments**.

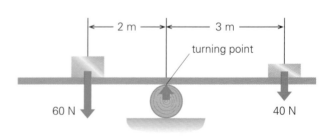

2 m

3 m

turning point

60 N

40 N

moment (to left)
= 60 × 2
= 120 Nm

moment (to right)
= 40 × 3
= 120 Nm

these are equal

Centre of gravity

Moments in balance

total weight of different parts = weight of whole body

centre of gravity

balanced   not balanced

All parts of your body have weight. Together, they act like a single force pulling at just one point. This point is called your **centre of gravity**.

To balance on a beam, as in the photograph above, you have to keep your centre of gravity over the beam. Otherwise your weight will have a turning effect and pull you over.

1 In diagram A on the right:
  a) which of the forces, X or Y, has the greater turning effect on the nut? Explain your answer.
  b) how could the turning effect of force Y be increased?
2 Diagram B shows a model crane. The crane has a movable counterbalance.
  a) Why does the crane need a counterbalance?
  b) Why must the counterbalance be movable?
  c) What is the moment of the 100 N force (about point O)?
  d) If the crane is balanced, what moment must the 400 N force have?
  e) How far from O should the counterbalance be placed?
  f) What is the maximum load (in N) the crane should lift?

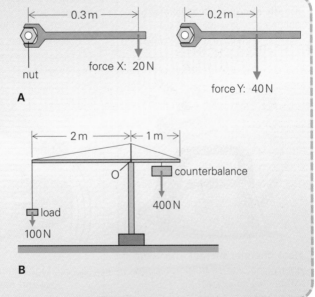

A

0.3 m — force X: 20 N

nut

0.2 m — force Y: 40 N

B

2 m — 1 m

O counterbalance

400 N

load
100 N

4.08 Energy

By the end of this spread, you should be able to:
■ *name a unit for measuring energy*
■ *explain what happens when energy changes form.*

You spend **energy** when you climb the stairs, lift a bag, or hit a tennis ball. Energy is spent whenever a force makes something move. The greater the force, and the further it moves, the more energy is spent.

Energy must also be spent to heat things up. Everything is made of tiny particles, such as atoms. These are constantly on the move (see Spread 3.01). To increase the temperature of something, it must be given more energy to make its particles move faster.

Forms of energy

Energy can take different forms. Here are some of the names used to describe them:

Kinetic energy This is the energy things have because they are moving ('kinetic' means 'moving').

Potential energy is stored energy. You give something potential energy if you lift it or stretch it. The energy is released when you let it go.

Chemical energy Foods, fuels, and batteries store energy in this form. The energy is released by chemical reactions.

Heat (thermal energy) This is the energy that comes from hot things when they cool down.

Light energy and **sound energy**

Electrical energy This is the energy carried by an electric current.

Nuclear energy This is energy stored in the nucleus of an atom.

Energy is measured in **joules (J)**.

On the right, you can see some examples of different amounts of energy. Large amounts are sometimes measured in **kilojoules (kJ)**. 1 kJ = 1000 J.

Energy chains

Just like money, energy doesn't vanish when you spend it. It just goes somewhere else! Below, is an example of how energy can change from one form to another. Scientists call it an **energy chain**:

In every energy chain, the *total amount* of energy stays the same. Scientists express this idea in the **law of conservation of energy**:

Energy can change into different forms, but it cannot be made or destroyed.

Typical energy values	
Potential energy:	
stretched rubber band	1 J
you, on top of a step-ladder	500 J
Kinetic energy:	
kicked football	50 J
small car at 70 mph	500 000 J
Heat (thermal energy):	
hot cup of tea	150 000 J
Chemical energy:	
torch battery	10 000 J
chocolate biscuit	300 000 J
litre of petrol	35 000 000 J

| chemical energy | → | kinetic energy | → | potential energy | → | kinetic energy | → | heat |

In any chain, some energy is always wasted as heat. For example, you give off heat when you exercise, which is why you sweat! However, the *total* amount of energy (including the heat) stays the same.

1. Give an example of something which has
   a) kinetic energy b) chemical energy
   c) potential energy.
2. A fire gives out 10 kJ of energy. What is this in joules?
3. What type of energy is supplied to a car engine? What happens to this energy?
4. Describe the energy changes that take place when you apply the brakes on a moving cycle.
5. Describe the energy changes which take place when you throw a ball up into the air.
6. Scientists say that energy can 'never be destroyed'. Explain what they mean.

Energy changers

Here are some examples of energy changers in action:

Energy input		Energy changer		Energy output
electrical energy	→	heating element	→	heat
sound energy	→	microphone	→	electrical energy
electrical energy	→	loudspeaker	→	sound energy
kinetic energy	→	brakes	→	heat

4.09 Energy on the move

By the end of this spread, you should be able to:
- *explain that heat is different from temperature*
- *describe how energy can be transferred by conduction and convection.*

KEY WORDS

heat   temperature   conduction   conductor
insulator   convection current

Heat and temperature

Everything is made of tiny particles. These are constantly on the move (see Spread 3.01). If something hot cools down, its particles lose energy. The energy given out is called **heat**.

Heat is not the same as temperature. The hot materials in the two photographs below are at the same temperature, but the amounts of energy they hold are quite different.

The sparks from these sparklers are at a temperature of 1600 °C. But they hold so little energy that they do not burn you when they touch your skin.

This molten (melted) iron is also at 1600 °C. It holds lots of energy and would be very dangerous to touch.

For heat to flow from one place to another, there must be a temperature difference between them. Here are two of the ways in which the energy can be *transferred* (moved):

Conduction

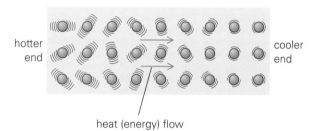

hotter end   cooler end

heat (energy) flow

If one end of a bar is heated, its particles vibrate faster. In time, their extra movement is passed on to particles right along the bar. Scientists say that energy is being transferred by **conduction**.

Metals are the best **conductors** of heat. Most nonmetals are poor conductors. Poor conductors of heat are called **insulators**.

Good conductors	Insulators (poor conductors)	
metals	glass	
especially	water	
silver	plastic	wool
copper	wood	fibrewool
aluminium	materials with air trapped in them	plastic foam
		fur
		feathers
	air	

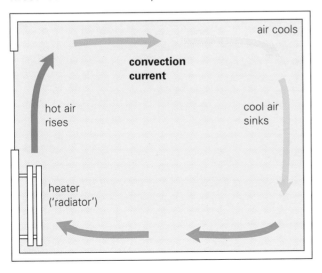

Air is a poor conductor of heat. Feathers, fur, wool, and plastic foam are all good insulators because they contain tiny pockets of trapped air.

Convection

If air is free to circulate, it can quickly transfer energy from one place to another:

When air is heated, it expands (takes up more space) and becomes less dense. It floats upwards because cooler, denser air sinks and pushes it out of the way. The result is a circulating flow called a **convection current**. Convection can occur in other gases as well as air. And it can occur in liquids, such as water.

Most rooms are heated by convection:

Convection has a part to play in the weather. You can see an example above. During the day, the land warms up more quickly than the sea. This sets up a convection current so that breezes blow in from the sea. Where warm, damp air rises and cools, clouds may form.

1 *conduction   convection*

   Which of the above processes is the reason for each of the following?
   a) The handle of a metal teaspoon gets hot if the spoon is left standing in a hot drink.
   b) In a room, the air near the ceiling is usually warmer than the air near the floor.
   c) If a canned drink is taken out of a 'fridge, the drink inside the can warms up.

2 Explain each of the following:
   a) In most saucepans, the base is made of metal, but the handle is plastic.
   b) Feathers, fur, and wool are good insulators.

3 Below, heat is flowing through a metal bar. The bar is made of tiny particles (atoms) which are vibrating. Which end of the bar has
   a) the higher temperature?
   b) the faster particles?

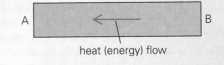

More energy on the move

By the end of this spread, you should be able to:
- *describe how energy can be transferred by radiation and evaporation.*

Energy can be transferred by conduction and convection (see Spread 4.09). Here are two more ways in which it can be transferred:

Radiation

On Earth, we are heated by the Sun, as shown on the right. The Sun's energy travels to us as rays of **electromagnetic radiation**. This includes **light** rays (which we can see) and **infrared** rays (which are invisible). If we absorb any of this radiation, it heats us up, so it is sometimes called **thermal radiation**. Often, people just call it 'radiation', although there are other types of radiation as well.

All warm or hot surfaces give off thermal radiation. The hotter something is, the more energy it radiates.

Giving off radiation	best – – – – – – – – – – – – worst

dull black	shiny black	white	silvery

Reflecting radiation	worst – – – – – – – – – – – best

Absorbing radiation	best – – – – – – – – – – – worst

Black surfaces are the best at giving off radiation. They are also the best at absorbing it.

Silvery or white surfaces are good at reflecting radiation – which means that they are poor at absorbing it. In hot, sunny countries, buildings are often painted white so that they absorb as little of the Sun's radiation as possible.

Silvery or white surfaces are also poor at giving off radiation. Kettles are usually made silvery or white so that they lose heat slowly.

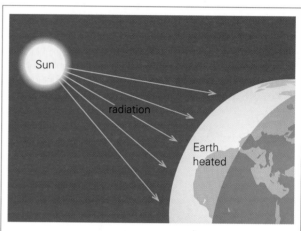

There is empty space between the Earth and the Sun. Energy can travel through space in the form of electromagnetic radiation. Moving away from the Sun, its heating effect is reduced because the radiation becomes more spread out.

The Sun's energy cannot reach us by conduction or convection because those processes depend on the movements of the tiny particles in a solid, liquid, or gas.

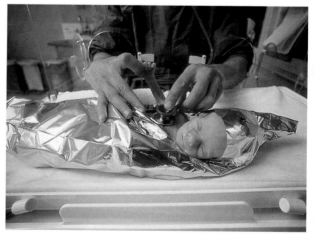

This shiny bag helps keep the premature baby warm. It reduces the amount of energy lost from the baby's body by thermal radiation.

The vacuum flask

A vacuum flask can keep drinks hot for hours. On the right, you can see the features which a flask has to reduce the amount of energy lost by conduction, convection, and radiation.

The flask can also keep chilled drinks cold because it is just as difficult for energy to flow in as out.

Evaporation

Wet hands dry out in a few minutes. This is because the water **evaporates** (changes into vapour). If air is blowing from a drier, as below, the water evaporates much more quickly.

As your hands dry, they feel colder. This is because energy is needed to turn liquid water into vapour. The vapour takes the energy from your hands, so they cool down. Overall, energy is transferred from your hands to the air.

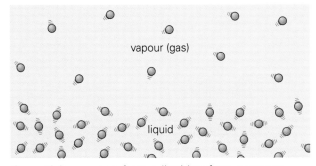

As particles escape from a liquid to form a vapour, they take energy with them, so the liquid cools down.

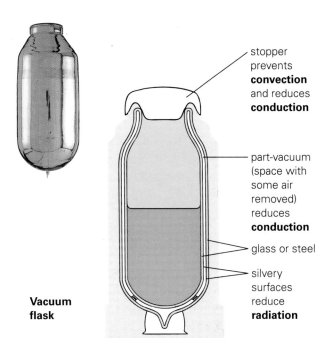

Vacuum flask

stopper prevents **convection** and reduces **conduction**

part-vacuum (space with some air removed) reduces **conduction**

glass or steel

silvery surfaces reduce **radiation**

To answer these questions, you may also need information from the previous spread, 4.09.

1 Explain why
 a) houses in hot countries are often painted white
 b) it is better for a kettle to be white or silvery on the outside rather than black.

2

If the cars above are left standing in a car park on a sunny day, which one would you expect to be hotter inside? Give a reason for your answer.

3 What features does a vacuum flask have to stop energy losses by **a)** conduction **b)** radiation

4 Why is a vacuum flask good at keeping drinks cold as well as hot?

5 *conduction convection radiation evaporation*

 Which of the above processes
 a) is the method by which the Sun's energy reaches the Earth?
 b) depend on the movements of tiny particles in a solid, liquid, or gas?

Supplying the energy

By the end of this spread and the next (4.12), you should be able to:

■ explain why the Sun is the source of most of our energy

■ describe what our different energy resources are.

Energy from the Sun

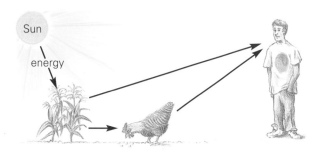

Plants get their energy from the Sun (see Spread 2.02). Like other animals, we get our energy by eating plants – or by eating animals which have fed on plants. So all the energy for our bodies comes from the Sun.

Our power stations, factories, homes, and vehicles need fuel. Oil (which contains petrol and diesel), natural gas, and coal are our main fuels. They are called **fossil fuels**. They formed from the remains of plants and tiny sea creatures that lived millions of years ago. So they store energy which originally came from the Sun.

> Most of the world's energy originally came from the Sun. To find out more, see the next spread, 4.12.

Turbine

Power stations

Mains electricity comes from **generators** in power stations. In most big power stations, the generators are turned by **turbines**, blown round by the force of high pressure steam. The steam is produced using the heat from burning fuel or from a nuclear reactor (see the diagram below).

In some power stations, the turbines driving the generators are turned by wind or flowing water. For more about this, see the next spread, 4.12.

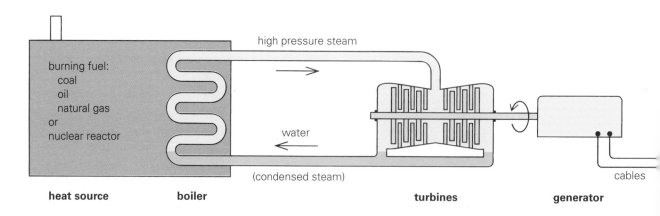

Renewable or non-renewable?

Fossil fuels (oil, natural gas, and coal) took many millions of years to form. Once used up, they cannot be replaced. They are **non-renewable**.

Some fuels are **renewable**. For example, if wood is burnt, it can be replaced by growing more trees.

Fuels like wood which come from plant or animal matter are called **biofuels**. The living matter itself is sometimes called **biomass**.

You can see some examples of renewable and non-renewable energy sources below. For more details on each one, see the next spread, 4.12.

Non-renewable energy sources	Renewable energy sources
fossil fuels: 　oil 　natural gas 　coal nuclear fuel: 　uranium-235	hydroelectric energy tidal energy wave energy wind energy solar energy geothermal energy biofuels (fuels from plant 　and animal matter)

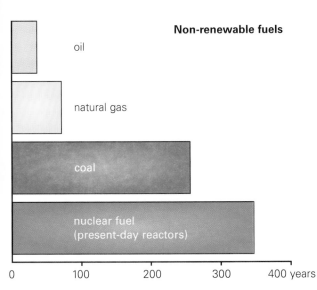

Non-renewable fuels

oil

natural gas

coal

nuclear fuel
(present-day reactors)

0	100	200	300	400 years

This chart shows how long the world's known reserves of non-renewable fuels might last if we go on using them at the present rate. It does not allow for the results of further exploration.

Wasting energy

We burn more fuels than we need to. Here are some of the reasons why energy gets wasted:

- People use lots of separate cars rather than a few buses or trains.
- There is traffic congestion.
- Some houses have wasteful heating systems and poor insulation.
- New materials and goods are often produced, when recycling old ones would save energy.

Unfortunately, some energy *has* to be wasted. When an engine (or power station) is burning fuel, less than a half of the energy released is used to produce motion (or electricity). The rest is lost as heat. This is not because of poor design. When a fuel burns, some of the energy released becomes so spread out that it cannot be changed into any other useful form.

Here are two good reasons for trying to be less wasteful with energy:

- Fossil fuels cannot be replaced.
- Burning fossil fuels pollutes the atmosphere and may be causing global warming (see Spread 2.15).

To answer the following, you will also need information from the next spread, 4.12.

1 What is meant by a non-renewable energy source?
2 Copy the table below. Write YES or NO in each blank space to show whether each fuel is a fossil fuel or not, and whether it is renewable or not.

Fuel	Fossil fuel?	Renewable?
wood		
coal		
alcohol		
oil		
natural gas		

3 Give *two* ways of generating electricity in which no fuel is burnt and the energy is renewable.
4 The energy in petrol originally came from the Sun. Explain how it got into the petrol.

How the world gets its energy

Solar panels
These absorb energy radiated from the Sun. They use it to heat water.

Solar cells
These use the energy in sunlight to produce small amounts of electricity.

The Sun
The Sun radiates energy because of nuclear reactions deep inside it. Its output is equivalent to 400 million billion billion electric hotplates! Just a tiny fraction reaches the Earth.

Energy in food
We get energy from the food we eat. The food may be from plants, or from animals which fed on plants.

Energy in plants
Plants take in energy from sunlight falling on their leaves. They use it to turn water and carbon dioxide from the air into new growth. Animals eat plants to get the energy stored in them.

Biofuels from plants
Wood is still an important fuel in many countries. When wood is burnt, it releases energy which the tree once took in from the Sun. In some countries, sugar cane is grown and fermented to make alcohol. This can be used as a fuel instead of petrol.

Fossil fuels
Oil, natural gas, and coal are called fossil fuels. They were formed from the remains of plants and tiny sea creatures which lived many millions of years ago. Industrial societies rely on fossil fuels for most of their energy. Many power stations burn fossil fuels.

Biofuels from waste
Rotting animal and plant waste can give off methane gas (as in natural gas). This can be used as a fuel. Marshes, rubbish tips, and sewage treatment works are all sources of methane. Some waste can also be used directly as fuel by burning it.

Batteries
Some batteries (e.g. car batteries) have to be given energy by charging them with electricity. Others are manufactured from chemicals which already store energy. But energy is needed to produce the chemicals in the first place.

Fuels from oil
Many fuels can be extracted from oil (crude). These include: petrol, diesel fuel, jet fuel, paraffin, central heating oil, bottled gas.

The Moon
The gravitational pull of the Moon (and to a lesser extent, the Sun) creates gentle bulges in the Earth's oceans. As the Earth rotates, different places have high and low tides as they pass in and out of the bulges.

Tidal energy
In a tidal energy scheme, an estuary is dammed to form an artificial lake. Incoming tides fill the lake; outgoing tides empty it. The flow of water in and out of the lake turns generators.

The atom

Some atoms have huge amounts of nuclear energy stored in their nuclei (centres). Radioactive materials have unstable atoms which release energy slowly. Nuclear reactors can release energy much more quickly.

Nuclear energy
In a reactor, nuclear reactions release energy from nuclei of uranium atoms. This produces heat which is used to make steam for driving generators.

Geothermal energy
Deep underground, the rocks are hotter than they are on the surface. The heat comes from radioactive materials naturally present in the rocks. It can be used to make steam for heating buildings or driving generators.

Weather systems
These are driven by the heating effect of the Sun. Hot air rising above the equator causes belts of wind around the Earth. Heat and winds lift water vapour from the oceans and bring rain and snow.

Wave energy
Waves are caused by the wind (and partly by tides). Waves cause a rapid up-and-down movement on the surface of the sea. This movement can be used to drive generators.

Hydroelectric energy
An artificial lake forms behind a dam. Water rushing down from this lake is used to turn generators. The lake is kept full by river water which once fell as rain or snow.

Wind energy
For centuries, people have been using the power of the wind to move ships, pump water and grind corn. Today, huge wind turbines are used to turn generators.

Sending sounds

By the end of this spread, you should be able to:
- say what causes sound and how it travels
- say how the speed of sound compares with the speed of light.

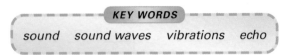
Making sounds

When a loudspeaker is working, its cone vibrates, and stretches and squashes the air in front of it, as shown on the right. The 'stretches' and 'squashes' travel outwards through the air as invisible waves. When the waves enter your ear, you hear them as **sound**.

Sound waves spread through air just as ripples spread across water. However, sound waves make the air vibrate backwards and forwards, not up and down. In diagrams, the 'squashes' are often drawn as a series of lines, as on the right.

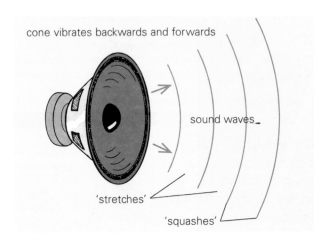

cone vibrates backwards and forwards

sound waves

'stretches'

'squashes'

Sound is caused by vibrations

In the loudspeaker above right, a paper cone vibrates. In your throat, stretched pieces of skin called vocal cords vibrate. Vibrations can also be produced by twanging, blowing, or hitting things. You can see some examples below:

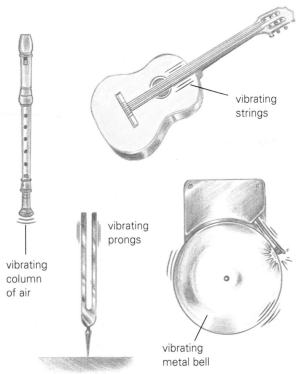

vibrating strings

vibrating column of air

vibrating prongs

vibrating metal bell

Sound needs a material to travel through

Sound waves can travel through solids and liquids, as well as gases. For example, sounds travel through walls and ceilings. You can also hear sounds when swimming underwater, and whales and dolphins use sound to communicate.

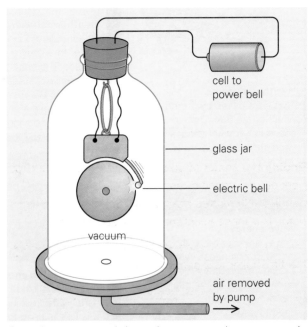

cell to power bell

glass jar

electric bell

vacuum

air removed by pump

Sound cannot travel through a vacuum (empty space). With no air to stretch and squash, there are no sound waves, and the bell is silent.

The speed of sound

In air, the speed of sound is about 330 metres per second. The exact speed depends on the temperature.

Sound travels faster through water than it does through air, and even faster through most solids.

Sound is much slower than light, which travels at 300 000 *kilo*metres per second. That is why you see a flash of lightning before you hear it. The light reaches you almost instantly, but the sound takes a little longer. For example:

If you see a flash of lightning, then hear the crash 3 seconds later...

The light arrives almost instantly.
3 seconds later, the sound arrives.
Sound travels 330 metres every second,
so, in 3 seconds it travels 3 × 330, or 990 metres.
So the flash was 990 metres away from you.

Sound is much slower than light, so you hear the crash after you see the flash.

Echoes

Hard surfaces, such as walls, reflect sound waves. When you hear an **echo**, you are hearing a reflected sound a short time after the original sound.

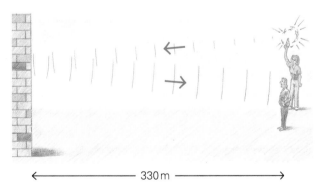

← 330 m →

Finding the speed of sound You can use an echo to work out the speed of sound. The girl above is standing 330 metres from a wall. She fires a starting pistol. Her friend hears the echo 2 seconds later.

The sound has travelled a distance of 2 × 330 metres. The time taken is 2 seconds. So:

$$\text{speed of sound} = \frac{\text{distance travelled}}{\text{time taken}} = \frac{2 \times 330}{2}$$

$$= 330 \text{ m/s}$$

Assume that the speed of sound in air is 330 m/s.

1. Give a reason for each of the following:
   a) You can hear sound coming from the next room, even though all the doors and windows are tightly shut.
   b) Sound cannot travel through a vacuum.

2. Leanne sees a flash of lightning, then hears the sound a little later.
   a) Why does she hear the sound after she sees the flash?
   b) If there is a 2 second delay between the flash and the sound, how far away was the lightning?

3. In the diagram below, Daniel shouts when he is 110 metres from a wall.
   a) What time does it take for the sound to reach the wall?
   b) When will Daniel hear his echo?
   c) If Daniel stands closer to the wall, how will this affect his echo?

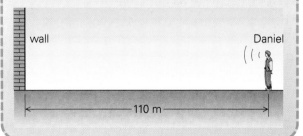

wall

Daniel

← 110 m →

Detecting sounds

By the end of this spread, you should be able to:
■ describe how the ear works
■ explain how hearing can be damaged
■ describe how sounds can differ.

The ear

Inside the ear, sound waves are detected and signals are sent to the brain for processing.

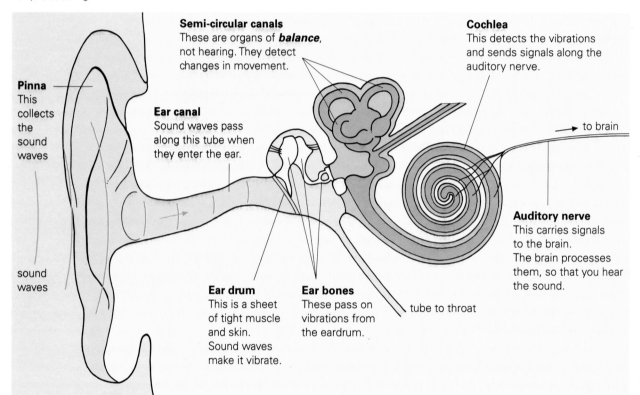

Semi-circular canals
These are organs of **balance**, not hearing. They detect changes in movement.

Cochlea
This detects the vibrations and sends signals along the auditory nerve.

Pinna
This collects the sound waves

Ear canal
Sound waves pass along this tube when they enter the ear.

to brain

sound waves

Auditory nerve
This carries signals to the brain.
The brain processes them, so that you hear the sound.

Ear drum
This is a sheet of tight muscle and skin. Sound waves make it vibrate.

Ear bones
These pass on vibrations from the eardrum.

tube to throat

Hearing problems

If the ear is not working properly, vibrations may not be reaching the inner ear, or signals may not be being passed to the brain. Here are some of the problems that can cause deafness or poor hearing:
● The ear drum may be damaged.
● Bone growth may stop the ear bones moving.
● The cochlea or auditory nerve may be damaged.

The cochlea and auditory nerve can be damaged by very loud sounds. That is why you should never play a personal stereo at high volume. If you are exposed to loud sounds over a long period of time, the damage may be so gradual that you do not notice.

Noise

Unwanted sound is called **noise**. It can be annoying. It can also be damaging. Scientists check noise levels using meters marked in **decibels (dB)**.

	Noise level in dB
personal stereo, very loud	150
damage to ears	140
rock concert	110
some ear discomfort	90
telephone ringing	70
normal speech	60
whispering	40

Sounds on screen

If you whistle into a microphone connected to a **cathode ray oscilloscope (CRO)**, a wavy line appears on the screen of the CRO, as shown on the right. You aren't really seeing sound waves. The up-and-down line is a graph showing how the air next to the microphone vibrates backwards and forwards with time.

Sounds different

Some sounds are louder than others. Some sounds are higher than others. With a CRO, you can see how different sounds compare.

Amplitude and loudness The height of a peak or trough on the screen is called the **amplitude**. The higher the amplitude, the *louder* the sound will be.

Frequency and pitch The **frequency** of a sound is the number of sound waves being sent out per second.

Frequency is measured in **hertz (Hz)**. If a sound has a frequency of, say, 100 Hz, then 100 sound waves are being sent out every second.

The higher the frequency, the higher the note sounds. Musicians say that it has a higher **pitch**.

If the frequency increases, you see more waves on the screen of the CRO. The peaks of the waves are closer together.

oscilloscope (CRO)

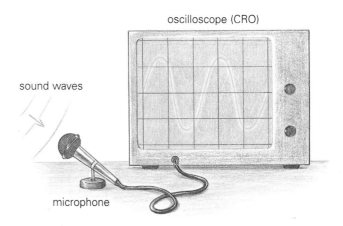

sound waves

microphone

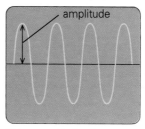 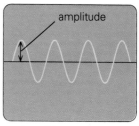

This sound is louder..... .....than this

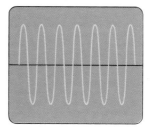 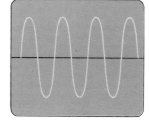

This sound has a higher pitch (and frequency)..... .....than this

---

1 cochlea   ear drum   ear canal
  Which of the above parts of the ear
  a) vibrates when sound waves strike it?
  b) sends signals to the brain?
2 Explain why a personal stereo played at high volume can damage your hearing.
3 The diagram below shows the traces made on the screen of a CRO by three different sounds. Which one **a)** is the loudest **b)** has the highest pitch **c)** has the highest amplitude **d)** has the highest frequency?

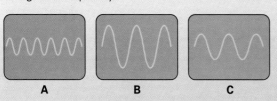

A   B   C

Frequency range The chart below shows the range of frequencies which can be detected by the human ear. The actual range differs from one person to another. For example, as people get older, their ability to hear high frequencies becomes less.

frequency		pitch
20 000 Hz	highest note heard by human ear	high
10 000 Hz	whistle	
1000 Hz	high note from singer	
100 Hz	low note from singer	
20 Hz	bass drum	low

4.15 Rays of light

By the end of this spread, you should be able to:
- explain why objects are visible
- describe how light can be reflected and refracted.·

Light is radiation which your eyes can detect. It normally travels in straight lines, as you can see in the photograph of the laser above. In diagrams, lines called **rays** show which way the light is going.

You see some things because they give off their own light: the Sun or a light bulb for example.

You see other things because daylight, or other light, bounces off them. They **reflect** light, and some goes into your eyes. That is why you can see this page.

The white parts of the page reflect light well, so they look bright. However, the black parts **absorb** most of the light striking them. They reflect very little. That is why they look so dark.

Transparent materials, like glass, let light pass through them. They **transmit** light.

Reflection

Most surfaces are uneven, or contain materials that scatter light. The light bounces off them in all directions. However, mirrors are smooth and shiny. They reflect light in a regular way.

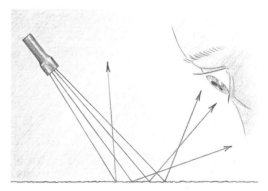

A rough surface scatters light – it reflects it in all directions. You see the surface because some of the light is reflected into your eyes.

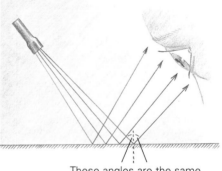

These angles are the same

Mirrors and other smooth, shiny surfaces reflect light like this. Each ray strikes at an angle and bounces off at the same angle.

 In space and in air, the speed of light is 300 000 kilometres per second $\longrightarrow$

Light is the fastest thing there is. It takes less than a millionth of a second for light to cross a room.

Image in a mirror

In the diagram on the right, light from a bulb is being reflected by a mirror. Some is reflected into the girl's eye. To the girl, the light seems to come from a position behind the mirror. That is where she sees an *image* of the bulb.

The image is the same size as the bulb, and the same distance from the mirror. However it is *laterally inverted* (back to front), just like these letters:

ЯOЯЯIM A NI ƎꓘIꓕ SꓘOO⅃ ⅁NITIЯW

Refraction

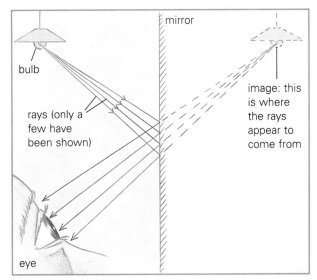

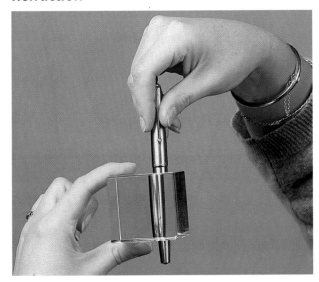

The light passing through the glass block above has been bent. The bending is called *refraction*: It happens with other transparent materials as well.

Below, you can see how a ray of light passes through a glass block. The lighted is refracted inwards as it enters the block, and outwards as it leaves it:

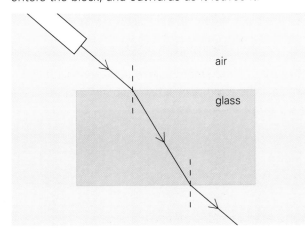

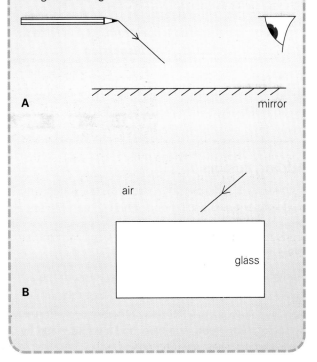

1 Hot, glowing things give off light. Explain why you can see this page even though it isn't hot and glowing.
2 Copy diagram A below. Draw in the rest of the ray to show how it will reflect from the mirror. On your diagram, draw in the position of the image of the pencil.
3 Copy diagram B below. Draw in the rest of the ray to show how it will pass through the glass block. On your diagram, label two places where light is being refracted.

A   mirror

air

glass

B

Seeing colours

By the end of this spread, you should be able to:
- *describe how primary colours can be added to produce different colours*
- *explain how objects give their colours.*

A spectrum

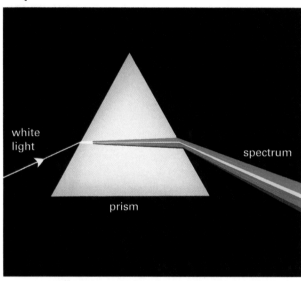

white light

prism

spectrum

White light from the Sun (or a bulb) is not a single colour, but a mixture of colours. These can be split up using a glass or plastic **prism**, as above. The light is refracted (bent) when it goes into the prism, and again when it comes out. The refracted light spreads to form a range of colours called a **spectrum**, as in a rainbow. The spreading effect is called **dispersion**.

In the spectrum, most people think they can see about six colours: red, orange, yellow, green, blue, and violet. But really, there is a continuous change of colour from one end to the other.

Adding colours

In the diagram above right, beams of red, green, and blue light are overlapping on a white screen. Where all three beams overlap, white is seen. To the eye:

red + green + blue = white

The white isn't a true white because some of the colours in the spectrum are missing. But the human eye can't detect the difference between a white made by adding red, green, and blue, and a white made by adding all the colours of the rainbow.

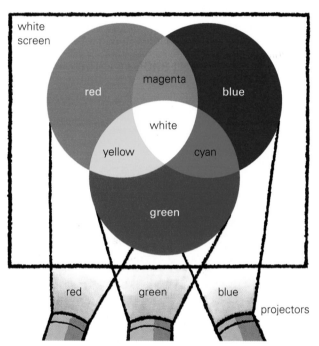

white screen — red — magenta — blue — white — yellow — cyan — green

red — green — blue — projectors

Red, green, and blue are called **primary colours**. These are colours which add together to make white. Where two primaries overlap, a new colour is seen:

red + green = yellow
green + blue = cyan
red + blue = magenta

The colours **yellow**, **cyan**, and **magenta** are called **secondary** colours.

By adding red, green, and blue light in different proportions, the brain can be given the sensation of almost any colour. On a TV screen, thousands of tiny red, green, and blue strips, glow in different combinations to produce a full colour picture:

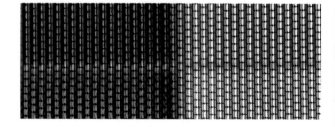

Taking colours away

The Sun gives out its own light, so does a TV screen. Most things are not like this. We see them because they reflect light from the Sun or some other source.

To the eye, white sunlight is a mixture of red, green, and blue. Things look coloured in sunlight because they *reflect* some colours and *absorb* the rest. In other words, they take colours away from white.

In white light:
- A *red* cloth reflects red light but absorbs green and blue.
- A *yellow* cloth reflects red and green light but absorbs blue.
- A *white* cloth reflects red, green, and blue. It absorbs no colours.
- A *black* cloth reflects virtually no light. It absorbs red, green, and blue.

Paints, inks, and dyes reflect some colours and absorb others. For example, red paint reflects red light, but absorbs green and blue.

When you mix coloured paints (or inks or dyes), the final colour is not the same as that produced by overlapping light beams. With overlapping beams, colours are being *added*. When paints are mixed, more colours are *taken away*, so less light is reflected.

The pictures in this book were printed using inks of just three colours: yellow, cyan, and magenta (with black added in places as well). For example, the red area in the 'overlapping beams' diagram was produced by printing magenta ink on top of yellow. Red light is reflected because it is the only colour not absorbed by either the magenta ink or the yellow.

Filters are pieces of plastic or glass which let through certain colours only. For example, a red filter *transmits* red light but *absorbs* green and blue, as shown below.

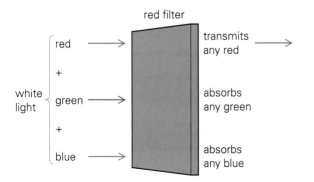

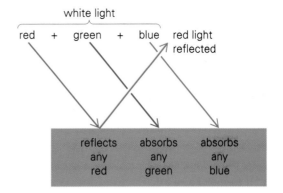

In white light, a red cloth looks red

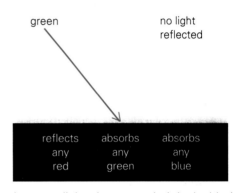

In green light, the same cloth looks black

▲ If you shine coloured light on something, its colour may change. There is an example of this above. A cloth which looks red in white light, looks black when viewed in green light. If green light only is striking it, that is absorbed, so no light is reflected.

1 What are the three primary colours?
2 What colour is produced when the three primaries are added together?
3 What colour is produced when red and green light beams overlap on a white screen?
4 What colours does a white coat reflect?
5 What colours does a black coat absorb?
6 **a)** What colour does a blue filter transmit?
  b) What colours does it absorb?
7 **a)** What colour does a green coat reflect?
  b) What colours does it absorb?
8 What colour will a green coat appear in red light?

Sun and Earth

By the end of this spread, you should be able to:
- *describe how the Sun appears to move across the sky through the day and in different seasons.*

KEY WORDS

star planet axis orbit day year

The Sun is a huge, hot, glowing ball of gas called a **star**. The Earth is a much smaller, cooler ball called a **planet**. The Sun is 150 million kilometres away from us. Other stars only look like points of light because they are a lot further away.

Day and night

The Earth slowly turns about a line called its **axis**. This runs from the North Pole to the South Pole.

It takes **one day** (24 hours) for the Earth to turn once. As it does so, places move from the sunlit half into the shadow half – in other words, from daytime into night. Viewed from the Earth's surface, the Sun appears to move across the sky as shown below.

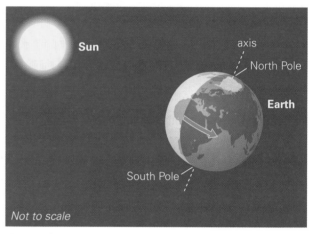

As the Earth slowly turns on its axis, one half is in sunlight while the other half is in shadow.

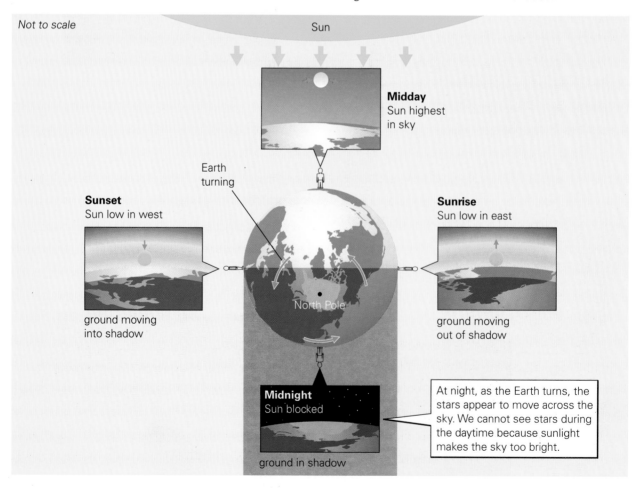

Midday
Sun highest in sky

Sunset
Sun low in west

ground moving into shadow

Earth turning

Sunrise
Sun low in east

ground moving out of shadow

North Pole

Midnight
Sun blocked

ground in shadow

At night, as the Earth turns, the stars appear to move across the sky. We cannot see stars during the daytime because sunlight makes the sky too bright.

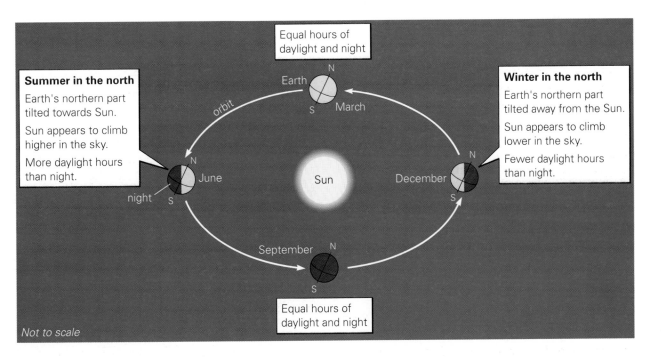

Equal hours of daylight and night

Earth

March

Summer in the north

Earth's northern part tilted towards Sun.

Sun appears to climb higher in the sky.

More daylight hours than night.

orbit

June

night

Sun

Winter in the north

Earth's northern part tilted away from the Sun.

Sun appears to climb lower in the sky.

Fewer daylight hours than night.

December

September

Equal hours of daylight and night

Not to scale

The year and seasons

The Earth moves around the Sun in a path called an **orbit**. Each complete orbit takes **one year** (about 365 days).

The Earth's axis leans by about 23°. As the Earth orbits the Sun, this means, for example, that the Earth's northern part is sometimes tilted towards the Sun and sometimes away from it. You can see this in the diagram above.

The diagram on the right shows the Earth in June, when the Earth's northern part is tilted towards the Sun. In Britain, for example, that is when the Sun appears to climb highest in the sky and there are most hours of daylight during each turn of the Earth. In other words, it is summer.

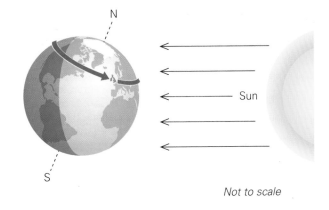

Not to scale

The Earth in June. Britain (in red) has more hours of daylight than night. Around the North Pole, there is no night at all: people see the Midnight Sun.

1 How long does it take for
  a) the Earth to turn once on its axis?
  b) the Earth to orbit the Sun?
2 **a)** Copy the diagram on the right. Shade in the part of the Earth that is in shadow.
  b) Write down whether it is *daytime* or *night* in Britain.
  c) Write down whether it is *summer* or *winter* in Britain.
  d) Explain why, in Britain, the Sun appears to climb higher in the sky in June than in December.

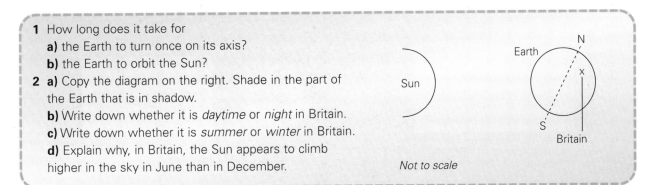

Sun

Earth

Britain

Not to scale

4.18 The Solar System

By the end of this spread, you should be able to:
- explain what the Solar System is
- explain how we are able to see the planets
- explain what keeps the planets in their orbits.

Planets in the Solar System

The Earth is one of many **planets** in orbit around the Sun. Many of the planets have smaller **moons** in orbit around them.

Together, the Sun, planets, and other objects in orbit make up the **Solar System**. This is too big for sizes and distances to be shown on the same diagram.

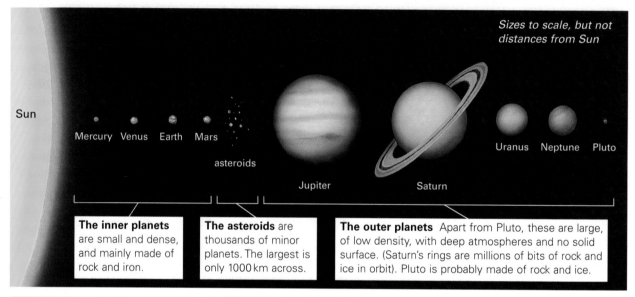

Sizes to scale, but not distances from Sun

Sun

Mercury Venus Earth Mars

asteroids

Jupiter

Saturn

Uranus Neptune Pluto

The inner planets are small and dense, and mainly made of rock and iron.

The asteroids are thousands of minor planets. The largest is only 1000 km across.

The outer planets Apart from Pluto, these are large, of low density, with deep atmospheres and no solid surface. (Saturn's rings are millions of bits of rock and ice in orbit). Pluto is probably made of rock and ice.

	Mercury	Venus	Earth	Mars	Jupiter	Saturn	Uranus	Neptune	Pluto
Average distance from Sun in million km	58	108	150	228	778	1427	2870	4490	5900
Time for one orbit in years	0.24	0.62	1	1.88	11.86	29.46	84.01	164.8	247
Diameter in km	4900	12 100	12 800	6800	143 000	120 000	51 000	49 000	2300
Average surface temperature	350 °C	480 °C	22 °C	−23 °C	−150 °C	−180 °C	−210 °C	−220 °C	−230 °C
Number of moons	0	0	1	2	16	23	15	8	1

stars

From Earth, a planet looks like a tiny dot in the night sky. Without a telescope, it is difficult to tell whether you are looking at a star or a planet.

planet

A planet is only seen because it reflects the Sun's light. Unlike a star, it is not hot enough to give off its own light.

Orbits of the planets

The planets have near-circular orbits about the Sun. This is how their orbits compare:

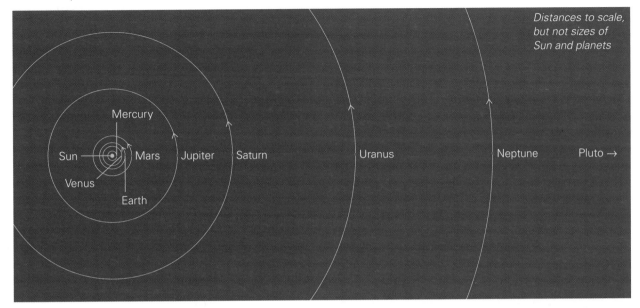

Distances to scale, but not sizes of Sun and planets

Gravity in action

We are pulled to the Earth by the force of gravity. No one knows what causes gravity. But scientists know that there is a gravitational pull between *all* masses:

● small masses have a weaker pull than large masses
● distant masses have a weaker pull than close masses.

The pull between everyday things is far too weak to detect. It only becomes strong if one of the things has a huge mass, like a planet. For example,

The gravitational force between a planet and the Sun holds the planet in orbit around the Sun. Without it, the planet would drift off through space. Similarly, the gravitational force between a moon and its planet holds the moon in orbit around the planet.

Beyond the Solar System

The Sun is just one star in a huge system of many billions of stars called a **galaxy**. In the whole **Universe**, there are many billions of galaxies.

Scientists think that other stars may have planets around them. However, most stars are so far away that their planets cannot be seen from Earth, even with the most powerful telescopes.

1 Which is the largest planet?
2 Which planets are smaller than the Earth?
3 **a)** Which planets are colder than the Earth?
   b) Why do you think that they are colder?
4 The diagram below shows the Sun and two of its planets (both have about the same mass).
   a) What is the name of the force that holds each planet in its orbit?
   b) Which of the two planets has the stronger force pulling on it?
   c) Which of the two planets takes the longer time to go round the Sun?
   d) From Earth, Venus looks like a very bright dot in the night sky. Why can Venus be seen, if it is not hot and glowing like a star?
   e) Carbon dioxide in Venus' atmosphere produces a severe greenhouse effect (global warming). What clues are there for this in the table on the opposite page?

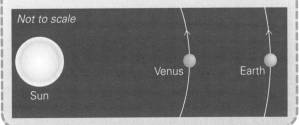

Not to scale

Satellites in orbit

By the end of this spread, you should be able to:
■ describe what satellites can be used for.

KEY WORDS

satellite   geostationary orbit   polar orbit

Satellites at work

There are hundreds of satellites in orbit around the Earth. Here are some of the jobs they do:

Communications satellites These pass on signals for telephones and TV.

If your TV is connected to a dish aerial, it gets its signals from a satellite like this.

Weather satellites These send pictures down to Earth (using radio signals) so that forecasters can see what the weather is doing.

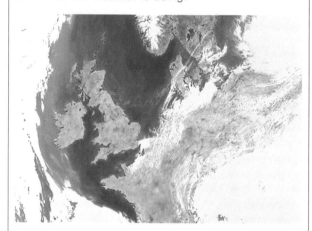

This picture was taken from a satellite. It shows the weather over Europe.

Research satellites Some of these carry telescopes for looking at stars and planets. Above the atmosphere, they get a much clearer view.

This is the Hubble Space Telescope. It uses radio signals to send its pictures back to Earth.

Navigation satellites These send out radio signals which ships, aircraft, or people on the ground can use to find their position.

This GPS (global positioning system) receiver picks up signals from GPS satellites, calculates its position, and shows the result.

Putting satellites into orbit

Satellites are launched into orbit by rockets, such as the Space Shuttle. For a low orbit just above the Earth's atmosphere, a speed of about 29 000 km per hour (18 000 mph) is required.

Communications satellites are normally put into a **geostationary orbit**, as shown on the right. The satellite orbits at the same rate as the Earth turns, so it appears to stay in the same position in the sky. Down on the ground, the dish aerials sending and receiving the signals can point in a fixed direction. For a geostationary orbit, a satellite must be 35 900 km above the equator and travelling at a speed of about 11 000 km per hour (6900 mph).

Satellites which survey the Earth are often put into a low **polar orbit** – one which passes over the North and South Poles. As the Earth turns beneath them, they can scan the whole of its surface.

A natural satellite – the Moon

The word 'satellite' really means any object which is in orbit around a planet. Most of the Earth's satellites are artificial (manufactured). However, one is natural – the Moon.

The Moon takes about 28 days to orbit the Earth. It also takes the same time to turn once on its axis, so it always keeps the same face toward us.

The Moon is smaller than the Earth (about a quarter of the diameter) and 380 000 km away. It has a rocky surface with lots of craters.

Unlike the Sun, the Moon is not hot and glowing. We can only see it because its surface reflects sunlight. And we don't see the part that is in shadow.

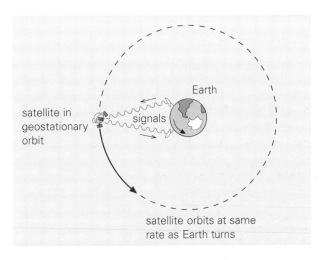

The Moon is a natural satellite of the Earth. When we look at its rocky, cratered surface, we only see the part that is reflecting the Sun's light.

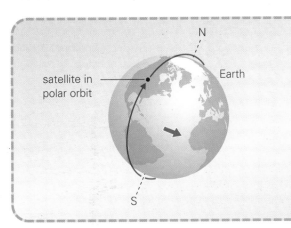

1 **a)** The survey satellite on the left is in a polar orbit above the Earth. For this type of satellite, what is the advantage of a polar orbit?
   b) Give *three* other uses of satellites.
2 Satellites that transmit TV pictures are in orbit and moving. Yet, down on the ground, the dish aerials that receive the signals point in a fixed direction. How is this possible?
3 **a)** We can see the Sun because it is hot and glowing. How are we able to see the Moon?
   b) Why do we sometimes see the Moon as a crescent?

Key ideas

The spread numbers in brackets tell you where to find more information

Cells in action

- Animals and plants are made of cells. Groups of cells form tissues. Collections of tissues form organs. *(2.01, 2.02, 2.04)*

- Different types of cell have different jobs to do. *(2.01, 2.02, 2.08)*

- In many plants and animals, a new life starts with fertilization, when a male sex cell combines with a female sex cell. *(2.03, 2.08)*

The human body

- Your body needs a balanced diet of carbohydrates, fats, proteins, minerals, vitamins, fibre, and water. *(2.06)*

- During digestion, food is broken down into materials which can be absorbed into the bloodstream. The blood carries these to the organs that need them. It also carries waste materials away. *(2.04, 2.06)*

- The body needs food for energy, growth, and repair. *(2.01, 2.04)*

- The skeleton supports the body, protects internal organs, and has joints for movement. Joints are moved by pairs of muscles. *(2.05)*

- Puberty is the start of the time when a girl can become a mother and a boy a father. *(2.08)*

- About once a month, a woman's ovaries release an ovum. If the ovum is fertilized by a sperm, it may develop into an embryo. *(2.08)*

- In the uterus, a developing baby gets food and oxygen from its mother's blood through the placenta and umbilical cord. *(2.08)*

- In the lungs, oxygen passes into the blood, and carbon dioxide and water are removed. *(2.07)*

- The body gets energy by aerobic respiration: food (glucose) is combined with oxygen, and carbon dioxide and water are made. *(2.07)*

- Smoking, alcohol, solvents, and drug abuse can damage your health. *(2.07, 2.10)*

- Most diseases are caused by germs (harmful microbes). Your immune system fights invading germs. Medicines and vaccines can also help. *(2.10)*

Green plants in action

- Plants use the energy in sunlight to change carbon dioxide and water into food (glucose) and oxygen. This process is called photosynthesis. *(2.02)*

- Plants need some of their food for growth. They also need nitrogen and other elements, which come from minerals taken in through their roots. *(2.02)*

- Plants need some of their food for energy. The energy is released during respiration. *(2.02)*

The variety of life

- Animals or plants of the same species (type) are not exactly alike. Some variations are inherited, others depend on the environment. *(2.12)*

- Animals, plants, and other living things can be classified into groups. *(2.11)*

- By selecting the parents carefully, animals and plants can be bred to give the characteristics that breeders want. *(2.12)*

Living together

- Humans grow crops, take materials from the ground, and burn fuels. These activities affect other living things. *(2.15)*

- To protect other living things and the environment, resources need to be developed in a sustainable way. *(2.15)*

- Different habitats support different animals and plants. *(2.14)*

- Animals and plants have to cope with daily and seasonal changes in their environment. They have become adapted to do this. *(2.14)*

- The size of a population is affected by competition for food and shelter, and the presence of predators. *(2.15)*

- Animals feed on plants and other animals. These feeding relationships are shown by food chains and webs. *(2.13)*

- A pyramid of numbers shows the numbers of animals and plants in a food chain. *(2.13)*

- Toxic materials can build up in a food chain. *(2.13)*

Key ideas

The spread numbers in brackets tell you where to find more information

Classifying materials

- Materials can be solid, liquid, or gas. *(3.01)*

- Different materials have different melting points, boiling points, and densities. *(3.01, 3.02)*

- Density can be measured in kg/m^3:

  $$density = \frac{mass}{volume} \qquad (3.01)$$

- According to the particle theory of matter, solids, liquids, and gases are made up of tiny, moving particles. This model can explain changes of state, gas pressure, and diffusion. *(3.01)*

- Everything is made from about 100 simple substances called elements. Elements are made up of atoms and can be represented by symbols. *(3.03)*

- All the elements are shown in the periodic table. *(3.13)*

- Different elements have different properties. Using these properties, they can be classified into two main types: metals and nonmetals. *(3.03, 3.13)*

- Elements can combine in chemical reactions to form new substances called compounds. *(3.03, 3.06)*

- Compounds can be represented by formulae, and reactions by word equations. *(3.03, 3.06)*

- In mixtures, the substances are not combined chemically. *(3.04)*

- Methods of separating the substances in a mixture include distilling and chromatography. *(3.05)*

Changing materials

- In a physical change, such as melting, the total mass of material stays the same. *(3.06)*

- When a substance dissolves in a liquid, a solution is formed. The solubility is a measure of the amount of substance which can dissolve. It depends on several factors, including the temperature. *(3.04)*

- Energy is needed to change a solid into a liquid or a liquid into a gas. *(3.02)*

- The surface of exposed rock is weakened by the weather. This is called weathering. Two causes are expansion and contraction as the temperature changes, and water freezing in cracks. *(3.14)*

- Some rocks form more quickly than others. *(3.15)*

- The three main types of rocks are igneous, sedimentary, and metamorphic. They are formed in different ways. *(3.15)*

- In a chemical reaction, the total mass of material stays the same, although the atoms become combined in a different way. *(3.06)*

- Most of the materials around us (and in our bodies) are formed by chemical reactions. *(3.12)*

- Chemical reactions are taking place whenever fuels burn, foods spoil, or metals corrode. *(3.09, 3.11, 3.12)*

- Burning fossil fuels damages the environment. *(3.09, 2.15)*

Looking for patterns

- Metals can react with oxygen, water, acids, and oxides of other metals. *(3.07, 3.08, 3.10, 3.11)*

- Metals can take part in displacement reactions. *(3.11)*

- Some metals are more reactive than others. This is shown in the reactivity series. *(3.10, 3.11)*

- Bases neutralize acids. A base which dissolves in water is called an alkali. *(3.07)*

- Solutions may be acidic, neutral, or alkaline. The pH scale is used to measure how strong or weak an acid or alkali is. *(3.07, 3.08)*

- If an acid reacts with a base, the products are a salt and water.
  If an acid reacts with a metal, the products are a salt and hydrogen.
  If an acid reacts with a carbonate, the products are a salt, water, and carbon dioxide. *(3.08)*

- Neutralization of acids by bases (and vice versa), has many uses, including the treatment of acid soil and the treatment of indigestion. *(3.08)*

- Acids in the environment can corrode metals and cause the weathering of rocks. *(3.11, 3.12, 3.14)*

Key ideas

The spread numbers in brackets tell you where to find more information

Electricity and magnetism

- For a current to flow in a circuit, the circuit must be unbroken. *(4.01, 4.02)*

- In a circuit, components (such as bulbs) can be connected in series or in parallel. *(4.02)*

- Ammeters are used to measure current, voltmeters to measure voltage. *(4.02)*

- In a series circuit, the current is the same all the way round. The more cells ('batteries') there are in the circuit, the greater the current. *(4.02)*

- In a circuit, the battery supplies energy, which is then spent in other components. *(4.02)*

- A magnet has a magnetic field around it, and poles near its ends. Like poles repel; unlike poles attract. *(4.03)*

- A current has a magnetic effect. This idea is used in electromagnets. *(4.03)*

Forces and motion

- Speed is calculated with this equation:

$$\text{average speed} = \frac{\text{distance}}{\text{time}} \qquad (4.05)$$

- Everything on Earth feels the downward force of gravity. This force is called its weight. *(4.04)*

- If the forces on something are balanced, its motion does not change. If the forces are unbalanced, it will speed up, slow down, or move in a different direction. *(4.04)*

- Frictional forces affect motion. *(4.05)*

- The turning effect of a force is called a moment:

$$\text{moment} = \text{force} \times \text{distance from turning point}$$
$$(4.07)$$

- If something is balanced, the total left-turning moment is equal to the total right-turning moment. This is the law of moments. *(4.07)*

- Pressure is calculated with this equation:

$$\text{pressure} = \frac{\text{force}}{\text{area}} \qquad (4.06)$$

- Pressure can be increased by reducing the area over which a force acts. It can be reduced by increasing the area. *(4.07)*

Light and sound

- Light normally travels in straight lines. *(4.15)*

- Most objects do not give off their own light. We see them because they reflect light into our eyes. *(4.15)*

- Mirrors reflect light in a regular way. *(4.15)*

- When light enters glass or other transparent material, it may be refracted (bent). *(4.15)*

- White light is a mixture of colours. *(4.16)*

- An object can appear different colours depending on the colour of the light striking it. *(4.16)*

- Sound waves make your ear drums vibrate. Loud sounds can damage your hearing. *(4.14)*

- Sound is much slower than light, and cannot travel through a vacuum. *(4.13)*

- Increasing the amplitude of a vibration increases the loudness of the sound you hear. Increasing the frequency increases the pitch. *(4.14)*

The Earth and beyond

- As the Earth rotates and orbits the Sun, the Sun's apparent position in the sky changes. *(4.17)*

- The planets orbit the Sun. They are held in their orbits by gravitational forces. *(4.18)*

- We see other planets (and moons) because they reflect the Sun's light. *(4.18, 4.19)*

- Satellites can observe the Earth and space. *(4.19)*

Energy

- On Earth, our energy resources include fossil fuels, biofuels, wind, and flowing water. Some are renewable, others are not. *(4.11, 4.12)*

- Most of our energy, including the energy in fossil fuels, originally came from the Sun. *(4.11, 4.12)*

- Electricity can be generated using many different energy sources. *(4.11, 4.12)*

- Heat flows because of a temperature difference. The energy can be transferred by conduction, convection, radiation, and evaporation. *(4.09, 4.10)*

- Energy can change into different forms. It is never lost, but can become less useful. *(4.08, 4.11)*

Periodic table

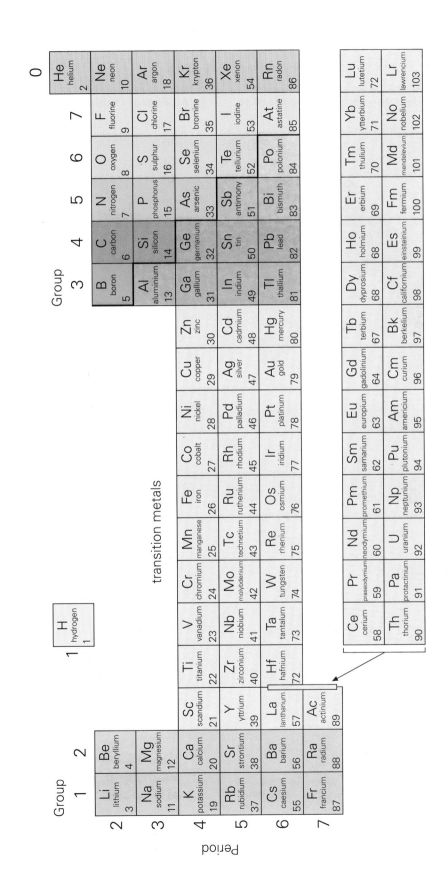

Test questions

Main test: 35 marks. Further (higher level) questions: 15 marks

1 The sparrowhawk (below) feeds on other birds.

a) Give *two* features of the sparrowhawk which help it catch and eat its prey. [2]

b) Give *one* feature which helps it cope with cold conditions [1]

2 Harry is working in the kitchen with his sister, Louise. Harry has a cold. Write down *three* ways in which Harry's germs might spread to Louise. [3]

3 The diagram below shows inside a human arm.

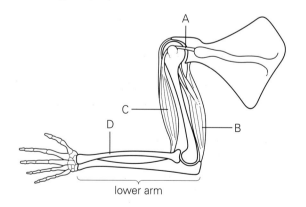

Four parts, A, B, C, and D, have been labelled.

a) Give one part which is made of bone. [1]

b) Give one part which is a muscle. [1]

c) Which part must contract (get shorter) for the lower arm to be raised? [1]

4 Many animals are vertebrates. Scientists classify these into five main groups.

fish amphibians reptiles birds mammals

a) What do all vertebrates have in common? [1]

b) Two of these animals are in the same group:

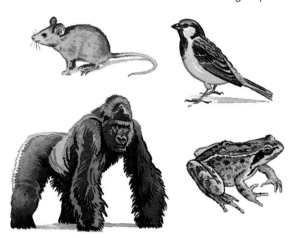

i) Which two are in the same group? [1]

ii) What group is it? [1]

iii) What feature made you put them in this particular group? [1]

c) Animals of the same species are not exactly alike. For example, cats have features which can vary from one to another. Give *two* reasons why two cats may look different. [2]

5 The diagram below shows a leaf cell from a plant.

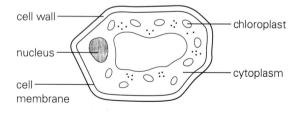

Several parts of the cell have been labelled. Which part(s)

a) is the cell's 'control centre' [1]

b) gives the cell a rigid shape [1]

c) is where photosynthesis takes place [1]

d) is *not* present in a root cell [1]

e) are *not* present in an animal cell? [2]

6 The diagram below shows the inside of the lungs. The lungs are filled with air, which is mainly a mixture of nitrogen, oxygen, water vapour, and carbon dioxide.

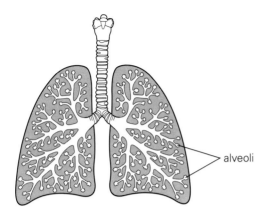

alveoli

a) Give *three* ways in which the air you breathe out is different from the air you breathe in. [3]

b) Explain why the alveoli are surrounded by lots of tiny blood vessels (tubes). [1]

c) Explain why, when you are exercising, you have to breathe faster. [2]

d) Give *two* ways in which smoking can have a damaging effect on your lungs. [2]

7

Vicky has a tree in her garden and some grass. The grass is much thicker and longer in the open areas than near the tree.

a) The tree has a large root system. Give *two* things which the tree must take in through its roots in order to grow properly. [2]

b) Give *two* reasons why the grass does not grow so well near the tree. [2]

c) During the autumn, the tree loses its leaves. Why does it do this? [1]

d) Give an example of how another form of wildlife (apart from grass) might be affected if the tree was cut down. [1]

8 These are the feeding relationships between some animals and plants in a large field,

snails feed on leaves
frogs feed on insects
insects feed on leaves
sparrows feed on snails and insects

a) Using the information above, copy and complete this food web by writing words in the blank spaces: [3]

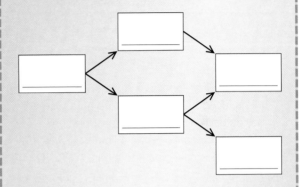

b) If the field is sprayed to kill all the insects, how will the following be affected? Give a reason for each answer:
   i) the population of frogs [2]
   ii) the population of sparrows. [2]

9 Plants make their food by a process called photosynthesis. Here are the substances involved:

oxygen   carbon dioxide   glucose   water

a) Which substances from those above must a plant take in for photosynthesis? [2]

b) Which substances are made during photosynthesis? [2]

c) Which substance is the food? [1]

d) Where in a plant does photosynthesis mainly take place? [1]

e) Why does photosynthesis take place in the daytime but not at night? [1]

f) During respiration, a plant 'burns up' its food in order to get the energy it needs. Using the substances listed above, copy and complete the following word equation to show what happens during respiration: [1]

_____ + _____ → _____ + _____

Test questions

Main test: 35 marks. Further (higher level) questions: 15 marks

1

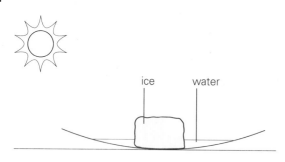

ice   water

a) In the diagram above, an ice cube has been left in a saucer out in the sunshine on a warm, dry day. Is each of the following happening?
i) A solid is changing into a liquid (YES/NO)   [1]
ii) A liquid is changing into a gas. (YES/NO)   [1]

b) *evaporating   freezing   melting   condensing*

Which of the above words describes each of the following?
i) A solid changing into a liquid
ii) A liquid changing into a gas
iii) A gas changing into a liquid.   [3]

2

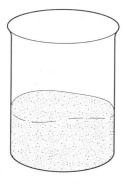

The beaker above contains a mixture of salt and sand. Describe how you would separate the salt from the sand.   [3]

3 Physical changes in materials are easy to reverse, chemical changes are not. Write down whether each of the following is an example of a *physical change* or a *chemical change*.
a) Boiling water changing into steam
b) A raw egg cooking and becoming hard-boiled
c) Wet cement drying and setting hard.   [3]

4 Adam used indicator paper to measure the pH of four liquids. Here are his results:

	pH
vinegar:	3
oven cleaner:	13
liquid soap:	8
kitchen cleaner:	11

a) Which liquid is the most acidic?   [1]
b) Which liquid is the most alkaline?   [1]
c) Which liquid would turn blue litmus paper red?   [1]
d) Wasp stings are alkaline. Which liquid would you use to neutralize a wasp sting?   [1]
e) If Adam measured the pH of pure water, what result would he get?   [1]

5 When Leanne heated some copper carbonate in a crucible, a chemical change took place. Here is a word equation for what happened:

copper carbonate → copper oxide + carbon dioxide

Here are the measurements Leanne recorded:

mass of crucible (empty) = 60.00 g

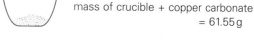
mass of crucible + copper carbonate = 61.55 g

mass of crucible + copper oxide = 61.00 g

a) Which substance in the reaction is a gas?   [1]
b) What mass of carbon dioxide was given off in the reaction?   [2]
c) In another experiment, Leanne burned some magnesium in the crucible and trapped all the solid material (magnesium oxide) that formed.
i) Write a word equation for the reaction   [2]
ii) This time, Leanne found that the crucible plus its contents weighed more after the reaction than before. Why was this?   [1]

6 Amin measured the solubility of copper sulphate in water at different temperatures. Here are his results, plotted as a graph:

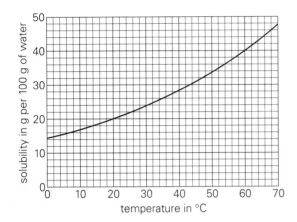

a) Describe how the solubility of copper sulphate changes with temperature. [1]

b) What is the solubility at 20 °C? [1]

c) How much copper sulphate can be dissolved in 100 g of water at 60 °C? [2]

d) How much copper sulphate can be dissolved in 200 g of water at 60 °C? [1]

7 Here are descriptions of four different rocks:

A Granite. This is made up of tiny crystals, formed when hot magma cooled.

B Basalt. This is made up of tiny crystals, but much smaller than those in granite.

C Limestone. This sometime contains fossils.

D Marble. This is formed when limestone gets heated in the ground.

a) Decide whether each of the rocks A to D is *igneous*, *sedimentary*, or *metamorphic*. [4]

b) Why are the crystals in the basalt smaller than those in the granite? [2]

c) The granite tor below has cracked and pieces have broken off. Why has this happened? [2]

8 Rachel tested four metals to see which ones would react with different solutions of metal nitrates. Here is her partly-completed table.

	zinc nitrate solution	copper nitrate solution	magnesium nitrate solution	iron nitrate solution
zinc		YES	NO	YES
copper	NO		NO	NO
magnesium	YES	YES		YES
iron	NO	YES	NO	

YES = reaction   NO = no reaction

a) Copy and complete the table. [2]

b) In the reactivity series below, the blank spaces are for the four metals in the table above. Use the test results in the table to decide which metal goes in each space. [3]

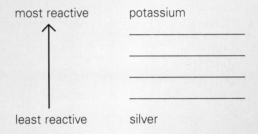

most reactive   potassium

least reactive   silver

c) Name a metal which will react with a solution of magnesium nitrate. [1]

d) Name a metal (apart from copper) which will *not* react with any of the solutions. [1]

9 Air is a mixture of substances. The table below shows some of them. All are made up of tiny particles (atoms or molecules):

substance	nitrogen	oxygen	water	carbon dioxide	argon	neon
chemical formula	N_2	O_2	H_2O	CO_2	Ar	Ne
boiling point, °C	-196	-183	100	-78	-186	-246

a) Which of the substances are compounds? [2]

b) Which of the formulae represent molecules? [2]

c) If warm air is cooled more and more, the substances in it eventually turn liquid. Which substance will liquefy i) first ii) last? [2]

d) Draw a diagram to show how the particles are arranged in
i) liquid water ii) water vapour (gas). [2]

Test questions

Main test: 35 marks. Further (higher level) questions: 15 marks

1

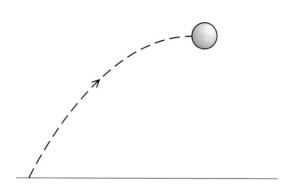

The diagram above shows a football travelling through the air after it has been kicked.

a) What is the name of the force that is slowing the football down? Copy the diagram and draw in an arrow to show this force. [2]

b) What other force is acting on the ball? Use an arrow to show this on your diagram. [2]

2 Matthew saw a flash of lightning. One second later he heard the crash of sound.

a) Why did Matthew hear the crash after he saw the flash? [1]

b) When Matthew saw another flash, there was a two-second delay before he heard the sound. What did this tell him about the lightning? [1]

3 Latha is carrying out tests with magnets and other materials to find out what magnetic forces there are between them. For each of the tests below, write down whether there is a force of *attraction*, or *repulsion*, or *no force*. [3]

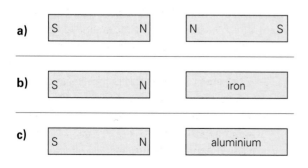

4

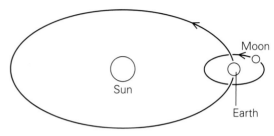

Not to scale

The diagram above shows the Earth orbiting the Sun (and the Moon orbiting the Earth).

a) What force holds the Earth in its orbit? [1]

b) Which object in the diagram is a star? [1]

c) Name another planet which also orbits the Sun, but closer in than the Earth. [1]

d) When viewed from Earth during the day, why does the Sun appear to move across the sky? [1]

e) As the Moon is not hot and glowing like the Sun, why are we able to see it at night? [1]

f) Copy the diagram above to show the position of the Earth 6 months later. (You can leave the Moon out of your diagram.) [1]

g) The Earth now has many satellites in orbit around it. Give *two* uses of these satellites [2]

5

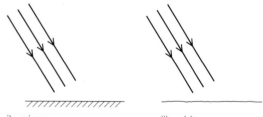

i) mirror   ii) white paper

a) Copy and complete the diagrams above to show what happens to the rays of light striking
i) the mirror [2]
ii) the white paper. [1]

b) In ii above, what difference would it make if the white paper was replaced by a piece of black paper? Explain your answer. [2]

6

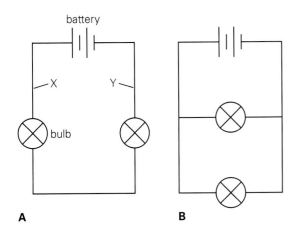

A **B**

Lauren wants to connect two bulbs to a battery. She tries two different circuits, A and B above.

a) When Lauren connects an ammeter into circuit A at point X, it read 0.1 A. If she puts the ammeter at Y instead, will its reading be *more*, *less*, or the *same* as before? [1]

b) Lauren wants to measure the voltage across the battery. Redraw circuit A to show where she should connect the voltmeter. [1]

c) Lauren finds that the bulbs in one of the circuits are brighter than in the other.
i) In which circuit are the bulbs brighter? [1]
ii) Why are these bulbs brighter? [1]

d) If one bulb is removed from each circuit, leaving a gap in the wire, how is the other bulb affected
i) in circuit A ii) in circuit B? [2]

7 This table shows some of our energy resources:

Energy resource	Renewable resource?	Energy originally from the Sun?
oil		YES
hydroelectric		
wind		
nuclear		
wood		
solar (cells)		

a) What is meant by a *renewable* resource? [1]

b) The energy stored in oil originally came from the Sun. Explain how the energy got from the Sun into the oil. [2]

c) Copy the table and complete it by writing YES or NO in each blank space. [4]

8

number of vibrations in one second ⇨ 256   256   288

A   **B**   **C**

Daniel wants to compare the sounds from three tuning forks, A, B, and C vibrating as shown above. He listens to the sounds one at a time.

a) Which tuning fork has the greatest amplitude of vibration? [1]

b) Which tuning fork has the highest frequency [1]

c) When comparing the sounds, what should Daniel do to make sure that his tests are fair? [2]

d) Listening to the sounds, how will the sound from B differ from that from A? [1]

e) How will the sound from C differ from that from A? [1]

9

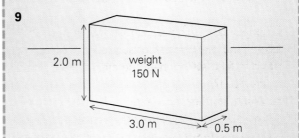

A large block of polystyrene weighs 150 N. It rests on the ground as shown above.

a) What does 'N' stand for? [1]

b) What is the area of ground under the block? [2]

c) What pressure (in N/m²) does the block exert on the ground? [2]

d) The block is tipped to a new position so that it exerts the least possible pressure on the ground. Draw the block in this new position. [1]

e) What pressure does the block exert on the ground in this new position? [1]

f) Use your ideas about pressure to explain why walking with bare feet on pebbles is more painful than walking on sand [2]

Answers to questions

1.02
1 87 mm 2 A 51 mm B 79 mm 3 225.2 g 4 76 ml 5 A 1.3 N
B 17.3 N 6 42 °C 7 X 3.3 A Y 0.76 A

1.04
1 a) Electric fire or hotplate b) X-ray machine 2 a) Plastics,
pesticides b) Catalytic converters, litter bins

2.01
1 a) choroplast b) cellulose c) cytoplasm d) membrane
e) nucleus 2 a) Energy, growth b) Eating plants or other animals
c) Make their own from simple substances 3 Cell wall,
chloroplasts 4 a) Collection of similar cells b) Organ

2.02
1 a) carbon dioxide b) oxygen c) oxygen d) carbon dioxide
2 glucose sugar 3 No light 4 Holes in leaves, letting gases in
and out 5 Absorbing water and minerals from soil 6 Plants
make oxygen

2.03
1 a) Ovules (in ovary, in carpel) b) Pollen (in stamens)
2 a) pollination b) germination c) fertilization 3 A fruit 4 a) To
attract insects b) Seeds are dispersed by animal droppings

2.04
1 a) brain b) heart c) stomach d) lung e) lung f) liver g) kidney
2 Oxygen, water, food 3 From kidneys through bladder, from
lungs when breathing out

2.05
1 a) Brain b) Heart and lungs c) Spinal cord 2 Support, allowing
movement 3 Allow bending, absorb jolts 4 a) Calcium
b) Collagen fibres 5 a) Fibres attaching muscles to bones
b) Fibres holding joints together 6 a) Muscles can only contract
b) Antagonistic pairs

2.06
1 a) Change food into liquid form – or break large molecules into
smaller ones b) Absorbed into blood c) Leaves body through
anus 2 a) For growth b) Making bone and teeth; a) Fish, bread
b) Cheese, milk 3 Helps food pass through system
4 a) Carbohydrates, fats b) Table to show the following:
carbohydrates in bread; fats in eggs, cheese, milk; proteins in
eggs, cheese, milk, bread; minerals and vitamins in all; fibre in
bread; water in milk

2.07
1 a) oxygen b) carbon dioxide (+ some water) 2 a) For blood to
absorb/release gases b) For gases to pass through easily
3 a) Glucose b) Carbon dioxide, water 4 Take in oxygen faster,
get rid of carbon dioxide faster 5 Lung tissue damaged, air
passages blocked with mucus

2.08
1 Egg cell; release of egg cell; cycle of egg cell release, uterus
lining growth, period 2 28 days 3 Passes out of uterus
4 Must meet sperm 5 Extra 'skin' forms round it 6 In testicles
7 Condom, diaphragm

2.09
1 Chemical instructions needed from both parents for full set

2 Bag of watery liquid 3 Organ which grows into uterus lining
where substances can pass between mother's blood and baby's
blood; cord carrying blood between placenta and fetus
4 & 5 Through placenta and umbilical cord 6 Turns head down;
for exit from uterus 7 Substances in mother's blood can get into
baby's blood

2.10
1 Contact, animals, droplets in air 2 a) viruses b) bacteria
3 a) You should not get the disease because your immune
system is ready to fight the germs b) Vaccine makes your
immune system produce antibodies to fight the disease
4 Exercise, have good diet, avoid smoking

2.11
1 a) Ticks to show the following: all have backbones; all have
lungs; fish, amphibians, and reptiles have scales; birds have
feathers; mammals have hairy skin; fish, amphibians, reptiles,
and birds lay eggs; mammals' young born alive; birds and
mammals have steady body temperature b) All are vertebrates
(have backbone) c) Fish, amphibians, reptiles, birds
d) Mammals; hairy skin, young born alive, mothers make milk

2.12
1 Height, weight, hair length 2 a) gene b) sperm, ovum
3 Sheep with long hair, racehorses 4 Ticks to show the
following: eye colour depends on genes, skin colour and body
weight depend on genes and environment

2.13
1 a) cabbage → caterpillar → thrush → fox b) cabbage
c) caterpillar, thrush, fox d) thrush, fox e) caterpillar, thrush
2 See pyramid example on p40 3 a) Octopus, crab, seal,
seagull; populations would fall b) Total amount of poison passed
on to fewer and fewer animals

2.14
1 a) environment b) habitat 2 a) Hibernates to reduce need for
food b) Loses leaves to reduce need for water 3 a) Large eyes
b) Large claws c) Sharp beak, large claws d) Feathers which
can trap air 4 a) Tides cover/uncover beach b) Temperature
changes from summer to winter

2.15
1 Not enough food, predators will eat rabbits 2 A Stop crops
being damaged by pests/pollute soil B Getting timber/destroying
wildlife habitats C Growing more crops/destroying wildlife
habitats 3 a) Cause injury b) Pollute soil 4 Sea polluted with oil
can kill seabirds

3.01
1 a) gas b) solid c) liquid d) gas e) gas 2 a) Particles from
perfume pushed around by particles in air b) Diffusion
3 a) 1000 kg b) 10 000 kg c) 78 000 kg 4 Collide with inside
surface and push it outwards

3.02
1 a) evaporating b) condensing c) melting d) freezing
2 Becomes water vapour (gas) in air 3 a) 0 °C b) 100 °C
4 a) mercury, water b) aluminium, iron c) tungsten d) mercury,
water, aluminium, iron, tungsten e) hydrogen, oxygen, methane
f) oxygen g) hydrogen

3.03

1 Metals, nonmetals **2** Aluminium, iron, calcium, sodium, potassium, magnesium **3** a) compound b) atom c) molecule
4 SO_2, C_2H_6

3.04

1 Single substance with nothing mixed in **2** a) water b) brine c) sodium chloride **3** a) Mixture of metal and other substance(s) b) Improved properties **4** a) 40g per 100g of water b) Increases c) 150g

3.05

1 a) Nitrogen b) Oxygen c) Oxygen d) Helium e) Carbon dioxide **2** a) Dissolving b) Filtering or distilling c) Chromatography **3** a) tea-bag (flavoured water, tea leaves) b) bag in vacuum-cleaner (dust, air)

3.06

1 a) With a magnet b) Iron and sulphur chemically combined and not affected by magnet c) Same **2** a) magnesium + oxygen → magnesium oxide b) magnesium oxide c) magnesium, oxygen d) magnesium oxide **3** a) and b) physical change (can be reversed) c) chemical change (cannot be reversed)

3.07

1 a) Dilute acid has more water in b) Strong acid more corrosive, lower pH **2** Hydrogen **3** a) Upturned test-tube b) Hydrogen c) Air-hydrogen mixture explodes with pop when lit **4** a) Red b) Blue **5** Acidic **6** Slightly alkaline **7** pH 7

3.08

1 a) salt, hydrogen b) salt, water, carbon dioxide **2** a) sulphuric acid + copper oxide → copper sulphate + water b) copper oxide c) copper sulphate **3** a) Adding lime to acid soil b) Neutralizing a wasp sting with vinegar

3.09

1 a) oxygen b) carbon dioxide c) oxygen d) carbon dioxide e) carbon dioxide f) carbon dioxide **2** a) Ash has extra weight of oxygen because oxygen taken from air when magnesium oxide forms b) Cuts off oxygen supply **3** Global warming, acid rain

3.10

1 a) Yes b) Yes c) Gold d) Hydrogen e) Oxygen **2** a) Aluminium is reactive so readily forms compounds in the ground b) Gold is unreactive, so doesn't form compounds in the ground

3.11

1 a) Iron has corroded because it has reacted in air and water, gold has not reacted b) Iron would not have reacted, so no corrosion **2** a) copper b) silver displaces copper c) copper + silver nitrate → silver + copper nitrate **3** a) No (copper less reactive than zinc, so doesn't displace it) b) Yes (zinc more reactive than hydrogen) c) No (copper less reactive than hydrogen) d) No (copper less reactive than zinc)

3.12

1 a) polythene b) alcohol c) iron d) wood **2** alcohol, cheese **3** a) Prevents fat becoming oxidized b) Rusting

3.13

1 metals – calcium, chromium; nonmetals – sulphur argon **2** Metals, very reactive **3** Gases, very unreactive **4** Silicon **5** neon – very unreactive gas; sodium – very reactive metal; nickel – magnetic metal

3.14

1 Expansion and contraction, frost, acid rain **2** a) Rock (or soil) being worn away b) Wind, sea, rivers **3** Rock underneath **4** Particles transported, deposited as sediments, crushed to form new rock

3.15

1 a) lava b) magma c) strata **2** a) igneous b) metamorphic c) sedimentary **3** Magma cools more slowly **4** Limestone usually formed from other fragments, granite formed from molten material **5** a) Shale (mudstone) changed by pressure into slate b) Shale was originally deposited in layers

4.01

1 a) copper, aluminium, carbon b) polythene PVC **2** No; circuit not complete **3** a) and b) bulb ON c) bulb OFF

4.02

1 Ammeter; 2.0 **2** Voltmeter **3** a) Brighter b) Higher c) Higher (approx double) **4** a) Reduced to original brightness b) Reduced to original value (2.0) **5** Brightness not reduced; one bulb keeps working if other bulb removed

4.03

1 a) S-pole b) S-pole **2** a) Increased b) Reduced c) Reduced **3** a) Input circuit can have small switch and thin wires because current is lower than in motor circuit b) Current through coil produces magnetic field which pulls iron lever down and closes contacts **4** Steel and iron balls attracted to magnet, but aluminium and copper balls don't move

4.04

1 a) newton b) Upward arrow c) 6N **2** a) Upward arrow b) equal

4.05

1 a) 10m/s b) 150m c) 20s **2** Head-down position, shaped helmet, smooth & tight-fitting oufit, streamlined bike (e.g no spokes) **3** a) Two from: brakes, tyres, steering wheel b) Two from: wheel bearings, moving parts of engine & gearbox, car body moving through air **4** a) Lower speed, streamlining body b) Lower fuel costs, less noise

4.06

1 a) newton, square metre, newtons per square metre, pascal b) N/m^2, Pa **2** a) Flat shoes have larger area in contact with ground, so pressure is less and shoes don't sink in so far b) Very sharp blade has smaller contact area, so pressure is higher and surface parts more easily **3** a) $4m^2$ b) $300N/m^2$ c) $200N/m^2$

4.07

1 a) Y; 40N × 0.2m is greater than 20N × 0.3m b) Move Y further from nut **2** a) To give turning effect which matches turning effect of load, so that centre of gravity of crane and load is over base b) When load is changed, turning effect of counterbalance must be changed c) 200Nm d) 200Nm e) 0.5m f) 200N (counterbalance is then at max distance)

4.08

1 a) Moving car b) Battery c) Stretched spring **2** 10000J **3** Chemical; changed to heat + kinetic energy **4** Kinetic → heat **5** Chemical → kinetic → potential → kinetic → heat **6** Energy can change forms, but total amount stays the same

4.09

1 a) conduction b) convection c) conduction 2 a) Base good conductor to let heat through, handle insulator to reduce heat flow into hand b) They trap air 3 a) B b) B

4.10

1 a) To reflect the Sun's thermal radiation b) To reduce loss of heat by thermal radiation 2 A; Black is the better absorber of thermal radiation 3 a) Part vacuum, stopper b) Silvery surfaces 4 Reduces heat flow in either direction 5 a) radiation b) conduction, convection, evaporation

4.11

1 Cannot be replaced 2 Table to show the following: coal, oil, natural gas are fossil fuels; wood, alcohol are renewable 3 Hydroelectric scheme, wind-driven generators 4 Ancient sea plants absorbed Sun's energy, ancient sea creatures fed on plants, remains of plants and creatures trapped and crushed by sediment to form oil, petrol extracted from oil

4.13

1 a) Sound can travel through solid materials b) There is no material to carry the vibrations 2 a) Sound much slower than light b) 660 m 3 a) $1/3$ s b) $2/3$ s after he shouts c) Less delayed (and louder)

4.14

1 a) ear drum b) cochlea 2 Loud sounds can damage cochlea and auditory nerve 3 a) B b) A c) B d) A

4.15

1 It reflects daylight or other lighting 2 Ray should reflect at same angle as it strikes; image is same position below mirror as pencil is above 3 Ray bends downwards slightly through block, then leaves block parallel to original direction; light is refracted where it enters the block and where it leaves it

4.16

1 Red, green, blue 2 White 3 Yellow 4 Red, green, blue 5 All 6 a) Blue b) Red, green 7 a) Green b) Red, blue 8 Black

4.17

1 a) I day b) 1 year 2 a) Right half of Earth is in shadow b) night c) winter d) Northern end of Earth's axis tilting towards Sun, so, viewed from Britain, the Sun reaches a higher angle above the horizon

4.18

1 Jupiter 2 Mercury, Venus, Mars, Pluto 3 a) Mars, Jupiter, Saturn, Uranus, Neptune, Pluto b) Further from Sun, so receive less heat 4 a) Gravity b) Venus c) Earth d) It reflects the Sun's light e) Venus hotter than Mercury, yet further from Sun

4.19

1 a) Travels over whole of Earth's surface b) Three from: navigation, communications, weather pictures, space telescopes 2 Satellites orbit at same rate as Earth turns 3 a) It reflects Sun's light b) Only part of sunlit half visible from Earth

Test questions (Section 2)

1 a) Sharp beak, large claws b) Feathers which can trap air 2 Sneezing into air, onto food, contact with saliva 3 a) D b) B or C c) C 4 a) Backbone b) i) mouse, gorilla ii) mammals iii) fur/hair 5 a) nucleus b) cell wall c) chloroplast d) chloroplast e) chloroplast 6 a) Less oxygen, more carbon dioxide, more water vapour b) So that gases can pass in/out of blood c) Take in oxygen faster, get rid of carbon dioxide faster d) Lung tissue damaged, air passages blocked with mucus 7 a) Water, minerals b) Less light, water and minerals taken by tree c) To reduce need for water d) Birds lose nesting places 8 a) Left-hand box – leaves; middle boxes – snail (top), insects (bottom); right-hand boxes – sparrows (top), frogs (bottom) b) i) population will vanish because of lack of food ii) population will drop because there is less food 9 a) carbon dioxide, water b) glucose, oxygen c) glucose d) leaves e) No light at night f) glucose + oxygen → carbon dioxide + water

Test questions (Section 3)

1 a) i) Where ice meets water ii) Where water meets air b) i) melting ii) evaporating iii) condensing 2 Add water to dissolve salt, filter mixture to remove sand 3 a) physical change b) chemical change c) chemical change 4 a) vinegar b) oven cleaner c) vinegar d) vinegar e) 7 5 a) carbon dioxide b) 0.55 g c) i) magnesium + oxygen → magnesium oxide ii) Oxygen taken in 6 a) Increases b) 20 g per 100 g of water c) 40 g d) 80 g 7 a) A and B igneous, C sedimentary, D metamorphic b) Molten magma cooled more quickly c) Heating/cooling has caused cracks, water has frozen and expanded in cracks 8 a) NO in all four blank spaces b) magnesium, zinc, iron, copper c) potassium d) silver 9 a) water, carbon dioxide b) N_2, O_2, H_2O, CO_2 c) i) water ii) neon d) i) and ii) Diagrams with particles as on page 46

Test questions (Section 4)

1 a) Air resistance (or friction), horizontal arrow from ball pointing to left b) Gravity, downward arrow from ball 2 a) Sound slower than light b) Further away (twice as far) 3 a) repulsion b) attraction c) no force 4 a) Gravity b) Sun c) Venus or Mercury d) Earth rotates e) Reflects Sun's light f) Earth at opposite point on its orbit g) Two from: navigation, communications, weather pictures, space telescopes 5 a) i) Rays reflect at same angle ii) Rays reflect in different directions b) No reflected rays; black absorbs light 6 a) same b) Diagram to show voltmeter connected across battery c) i) B ii) They each get full battery voltage d) i) Goes off ii) Stays on 7 a) Can be replaced when used up b) Ancient sea plants absorbed Sun's energy, ancient sea creatures fed on plants, remains of plants and creatures trapped and crushed by sediment to form oil c) Table to show the following: all except oil and nuclear are renewable; all except nuclear got energy from Sun 8 a) B b) C c) Ear same distance from each fork, fork in same position with same reflecting surfaces around it d) Louder e) Higher pitch 9 a) newton b) 1.5 m² c) 100 N/m² d) Diagram to show block resting on 2.0 m × 3.0 m face e) 25 N/m² f) Pebbles reduce area in contact with feet, so those parts of the feet feel a higher pressure

Index

absolute zero 49
acid-carbonate reactions 61
acid-metal reactions 61
acid rain 61, 72
acids 58–61
acids, reactions with carbonates 61
acids, reactions with metals 61, 65
adapted for living 42–43
AIDS 29
aerobic respiration 19, 28
air, gases in 54
air resistance 82–83, 85
alcohol, making 69
alkalis 58–60
alveoli 28
alloys 53
aluminium, extracting 68
amylase 26
ammeter 78
ammonia 58–59
ampere (A) 78
amphibians 36–37
amplitude (sound waves) 103
animals, classifying 36–37
antibiotics 14, 35
asteroids 110
atomic number 71
atoms, charges in 76
atoms, particles in 71, 76
atoms and elements 71
atoms in molecules 50–51

baby, birth of 32–33
bacteria 34–35
bases (chemical) 58–61
battery 77
Big Bang 13
biofuels 97–98
biomass 97
birds 36–37
birth 33
birth control 31
bladder 23
blood 22
blood vessels 22
boiling 48–49
boiling point 49
bone 24
brain 23, 25
breathing 29
burning 62–63

capillaries, blood 22, 28
carbohydrates 27
carbon dioxide and living things 18–19
carbon dioxide in air 45, 54
carbon dioxide, testing for 54
carbonates, reaction with acids 61
catalysts 15
cells, animal and plant 16–17
cells, electric 77–78
cells, in leaves and roots 18
cells, sex (flowers) 20
cells, sex (humans) 30–31, 39
cellulose 17
Celsius scale 49

centre of gravity 89
charge, electric 76
characteristics (living things) 38–39
chemical change 56
chemical reaction 56
chlorophyll 17
chloroplasts 17
chromatography 55
chromosomes 16, 38
cilia 28
circuit breaker 81
circuits, electric 77–79
circuits, series and parallel 79
classifying living things 36–37
coal 63, 97–98
colour 106–107
combustion 62–63
compass 80
compounds 51
condensing 48
conduction of heat 92–93
conductors, electrical 76
conductors, heat 92
consumers (in food chain) 40
contraception 31
convection 93
corrosion 67
crust, Earth's 74
crystallizing 55
current 76, 78
current, magnetic effect 80–81

day and night 108
decomposers 40, 69
density 47
deposition (rock fragments) 73
diet 26–27, 35
diffusion 46
digestion 26
disease 34–35
dispersal of seeds 21
dispersion of light 106
displacement reaction 66
dissolving 52
distilling 54–55
DNA 38

ear, human 102
Earth and planets 12, 108–111
Earth, structure 74
echoes 101
electric charge 76
electric current *see* current
electricity 76–81
electricity, generating 96, 99
electromagnets 80–81
electrons in atom 71, 76
elements 50–51, 70–71
embryo, human 32
energy, sources 97–99
energy, forms and conservation 90–91
energy, renewable and non-renewable 97
energy from the Sun 96–99
energy, wasting 97
environment (of living things) 38, 42
enzymes, digestive 26

enzymes, using 68–69
erosion 73
evaporation 48, 55
evaporation, energy transfer by 95

fair test 8
fats 27
fermentation 69
fertilization (in flowers) 21
fertilization (in humans) 30–31
fetus 33
fibre (in food) 27
filtering 55
filters, colour 107
fish 36–37
flowers 20–21
food chains and webs 40–41
food, making and using 18–19
food, digestion of 26
food, substances in 27
forces 82–89
force, turning effect of 88–89
forces, balanced and unbalanced 83
formula, chemical 51
fossil fuels 63, 97–98
freezing 48
frequency (sound) 103
friction 84–85
fruits 21
fuels, burning 62–63
fungi 34, 37

galaxies 12–13, 111
gas, natural 63, 97–98
gas, particles in 46–48
genes 38–39
genetic modification 39
germination 21
germs 34–35
global warming 45
glucose, made in plants 18
glucose in respiration 19, 28, 62
gravity and weight 82
gravity and planets 111
gut 23, 26

habitat 42
health 33, 34–35
heart 23
heat 92
hertz (Hz) 103
HIV 35
hydroelectric energy 99
hydrogen from reactions 58, 64–65
hydrogen, testing for 58

igneous rocks 74
image in mirror 105
immune system 35
indicators 59
infections 34
inherited characteristics 38–39
insects 37
insulators, electrical 76
insulators, heat 92–93
iron, corrosion of 67

iron, extracting 68

joints (in skeleton) 24–25
joule (J) 91

Kelvin scale 49
key factors 8
kidneys 23
kilogram (kg) 47
kingdoms (living things) 36–37

lasers 14, 104
lava 74
leaves 18–19
light 104–107
light, speed of 101, 104
limestone 61, 75
line of best fit (graph) 9
liquid, particles in 46, 48
litmus 59
liver 23
loudness 103
lungs 23, 28–29

magma 74
magnetic fields 80
magnets 80
mammals 36–37
mantle, Earth's 74
mass 47
melting 48–49
melting point 49
menstrual cycle 30
metals and reactivity 64–67
metals, extracting 68
metals, magnetic 70, 81
metals in periodic table 70–71
metals, properties of 50, 64–67, 81
metamorphic rocks 75
microbes and disease 34
microbes, using 69
mineral (meaning) 72
minerals in food 27
minerals in soil 18
mirrors (flat) 104–105
mixtures 52–55
mixtures, separating 55
model, scientific 12
molecules 51
moments (of forces) 88–89
Moon 113
moons 110
muscles 23, 25

natural gas 63, 97–98
nerves and nervous system 25
neutralization 58, 60
newton (N) 82
nitrates 18
nitrogen in air 54
nitrogen for plants 18
nitrogen, uses of 54, 69
noise 102
nonmetals, properties of 50
nonmetals in periodic table 70–71
nuclear energy 99
nucleus of atom 71, 76
nucleus of cell 16–17

oil for plastics 68
oil for fuels 63, 97–98
orbits of Earth and planets 12, 109, 111
orbits of satellites 113
ores 65, 68
organ (meaning) 17
organs in human body 23
ovary (in flower) 20–21
ovary (in human) 30
ovules (in flower) 20
ovulation 30
ovum 30–32, 39
oxidation of food 69
oxide 62
oxygen and living things 18–19
oxygen, competing for 66
oxygen in air 54
oxygen, testing for 63

parallel circuits 79
particle theory of matter 46, 51
pascal (Pa) 86
periodic table 70–71, 117
pH scale 59
photosynthesis 18–19
physical change 57
pitch (sound) 103
placenta 32–33
planets 110–111
planets, early ideas 12
plants, classifying 36-37
plastics 15, 68
poles, magnetic 80
pollen and pollination 20–21
pollution 45, 63
pollution in food chain 41
populations, growth and limit 44
power stations 96, 99
predators 40, 44
pressure 86–87
pressure from particles in a gas 47
prey 40
prism 106
producer (in food chain) 40
product of a reaction 56
proteins in food 27
puberty 30
pyramid of numbers 40

radiation, thermal (heat) 94–95
rays of light 104–105
reactant 56
reaction, chemical 56
reactivity 64–67
reactivity series 65–66
reflection of light 104–105
refraction of light 105
relay, magnetic 81
reproduction (flowering plants) 20–21
reproduction (human) 30–33
reptiles 36–37
respiration in plants and animals 19, 62
respiration in human body 28, 62
rock, recycling of 73
rocks, formation and types 74–75
rust 67

salts and acids 58, 60–61
satellites 112–113

seasons 109
sediment 73
sedimentary rocks 75
seeds 20, 21
selective breeding 39
semiconductors 76
series circuits 78–79
sex cells see cells
sex systems, male and female 30–31
skeleton, human 24
skin 23
smoking, effects of 29, 33, 35
soil 18, 73
Solar System 110–111
solid, particles in 46
solubility 53
solute 52
solutions 52–53
solvents 52
sound 100–103
sound, speed of 101
sound waves 100, 103
species 36
spectrum 106
speed 84
sperm 30–31, 39
starch in food 27
starch in leaves 19
stars 12–13, 111
state, changing 48-49
steel 53, 67
stomach 23, 26
strata, rock 75
Sun (star) 12, 108–110
Sun, energy from 96–99
sustainable development 44
switch 77
symbols, circuit 79
symbols for elements 50, 117

teeth 24
temperature 49, 92
tissue 17

umbilical cord 32–33
Universe 12–13, 111
uterus 30, 32–33

vaccines 35
variation in living things 38–39
vertebral column (backbone) 24
vertebrates 36–37
viruses 34–35
vitamins 27
volt (V) and voltage 78
voltmeter 78
volume 47

water, effect on rocks 72
water, molecules of 51
water, changing state 48–49
water, reactions with metals 64
weathering of rocks 72–73
weight 82
wind energy 99
womb see Uterus
word equation 56

year 109